The Insightful Teacher

Reflective Strategies to Shape Your Early Childhood Classroom

Nancy Bruski

Dedication

To my father, my biggest admirer, who always felt I was smarter and more wonderful than I am. I know you're smiling right now, somewhere in the cosmos.

To my husband, Mitchell, whose love, support, encouragement, and belief in my talents have been unwavering.

And to my children, Katy and James, who have taught me so much about what it means to be emotionally available. Thank you for giving me so many opportunities to grow. You will always be my proudest accomplishment.

Acknowledgements

First, thanks go to Kathy Charner for encouraging me to write a book! She helped me overcome my hesitation and fulfill my dream of becoming a published author.

Thanks to Adele Faber and Elaine Mazlish for their wonderful parenting books that I have found so helpful over the years! They have been mentors.

Vivian Paley's beautiful writing and unerring commitment to respecting the integrity of children have been an inspiration.

Elizabeth Jacob and Judy Bertacchi from the Virginia Frank Child Development Center inspired me to work with young children and allowed me to spend two years in the therapeutic classroom.

Thanks to my longtime friend and colleague Teri Talan for bringing me to Evanston Day Nursery, where I honed my skills and developed strategies that support social-emotional success.

Thanks to colleagues who have believed in and supported my work: Chris Baer, Lana Weiner, Debra Gaetano, Deborah Jobst, Sheila Maloney, Sharyl Robin, Marilyn Peterson, Gail Reichlin, Naomi Brackett, Leah Gibbons, and Susan Smith.

Finally, thanks to my dear friends, without whose steadfast support, encouragement, kindness, and patience I never would have finished this project: Roberta Rakove, Ronna Stamm, Maryjo Barrett, Karen Barrie, and Galienne Eriksen.

The Insightful TEACHER

Reflective Strategies to Shape Your Early Childhood Classroom

NANCY BRUSKI

Gryphon House, Inc.   Lewisville, NC

Copyright

© 2013 Nancy Bruski

Published by Gryphon House, Inc.
P. O. Box 10, Lewisville, NC 27023
800.638.0928; 877.638.7576 (fax)
Visit us on the web at www.gryphonhouse.com.

Library of Congress Cataloging-in-Publication Data

The cataloging-in-publication data will be registered with the Library of Congress for ISBN 978-0-87659-323-3.

Bulk Purchase

Gryphon House books are available for special premiums and sales promotions as well as for fund-raising use. Special editions or book excerpts also can be created to specifications. For details, contact the Director of Marketing at Gryphon House.

Disclaimer

Gryphon House, Inc., cannot be held responsible for damage, mishap, or injury incurred during the use of or because of activities in this book. Appropriate and reasonable caution and adult supervision of children involved in activities and corresponding to the age and capability of each child involved are recommended at all times. Do not leave children unattended at any time. Observe safety and caution at all times.

Table of Contents

Introduction

I read a wonderful book by Paul Tough, a former editor of *The New York Times Magazine* and noted journalist, titled *How Children Succeed: Grit, Curiosity, and the Hidden Power of Character.* I was intrigued by a review I had read of the book and by all the buzz in the educational field about how character relates to success in school and in life. In his book, Tough argues that improving children's cognitive skills is not enough to help them be successful learners. He reviews research that describes how traits such as resilience, integrity, resourcefulness, optimism, and ambition are critical components of helping children succeed long term. Tough states that these skills can be developed even in children who have not had support at a young age, and he focuses on programs around the country that work with adolescents to help them develop these traits that enable them to succeed.

My immediate reaction to reading this was that it is much better for children to have such experiences in preschool! It is difficult to overestimate the contribution that preschool teachers make to children's lives when they understand that learning numbers and letters is only part of the preparation for elementary school. Teachers also must focus on helping children learn to get along with one another, encouraging children to engage deeply in curriculum that challenges and appeals to them, showing them how to persist in problem solving, supporting them as they learn to resolve conflicts, and helping them comfortably accept differences in personality, skill level, and culture or race.

Children develop resilience through valuing themselves and having the inner strength and strategies to face challenges of all sorts. True self-esteem and confidence arise out of feeling personally validated and understood. *The Insightful Teacher* provides a holistic approach to developing classroom communities in which each child feels recognized, appreciated, and able to contribute in his own way. This book gives teachers the tools and strategies they need to help children build critical character traits and enable them to function successfully in the classroom.

One goal of a successful educational experience is to provide support for children to learn how to cope with, survive, and overcome disappointing experiences. Everyone experiences failure at some point. How people react to challenges defines their ultimate success, and the social skills and personal validation that preschool teachers offer to young children will help them keep moving forward in their lives.

The teacher's ability to reflect on her interventions in the classroom is an essential component of helping children develop self-confidence and self-control. Examining not only children's behaviors but also her responses to them will enable the teacher to tune in to children's needs and to develop ways of communicating with them that will promote growth.

This book will be useful for individual teachers interested in improving their practice, for directors to use for staff development, as a supplement to workshops or in-service training, or for college classes focusing on guidance with the young child. Each chapter is filled with examples from real classrooms and includes effective interventions from teachers, along with commentary and analysis. The chapters include journaling activities so that teachers can reflect on what they have read and how they might integrate the information into their practice.

It is my hope that teachers will feel excited and ready to implement this approach in their classrooms as they provide children with a baseline of emotional and psychological strength. In so doing, they will equip children with the skills to succeed in school and to face and overcome life's many challenges.

The Insightful Teacher

Supporting children's appropriate behavior at school begins with the teacher. Although this might seem counterintuitive, the teacher's perspective, approach, and values are the basis for creating a supportive, nurturing classroom and for shaping children's behavior. Understanding the child is necessary for encouraging that child to behave appropriately and function at her highest potential; however, the teacher first must reflect on and understand her own thoughts, feelings, and perspectives. Consider the following questions:

- What are my values as a teacher?
- What are my goals?
- What are my strengths?
- What are my weaknesses?
- What should an early childhood classroom look like?
- What behaviors are acceptable to me and which ones are not?
- What situations really challenge me?
- How do I usually respond to challenging situations, and do I need to do something differently?
- How do I engage the children in the learning process?
- How do I use the physical space in the classroom to encourage engagement and independence in the children?
- How do my interactions with the children reflect my goals, values, and perspective?

The reflective teacher is willing to examine her choices to gain insight. She looks at children's behavior as a mutual interaction, one that is composed not only of what the child does but also of what she may or may not have done before and after the child acted. Teaching affords wonderful opportunities each day for improving one's professional excellence through thoughtful interactions with children, creative planning and implementation, enthusiastic sharing of a personal experience or interest with the children, and a myriad of other possibilities.

Identifying Values and Setting Goals

Clarifying what one values in the classroom setting means answering some important questions.

- **What do I want to happen in my classroom?** For example, do I want the children to feel comfortable, safe, and free to explore? Am I comfortable with noise and activity, or am I more comfortable with the quiet hum of exploration?
- **What are my goals?** For example, do I want to communicate a welcoming atmosphere by checking in with each child every day? Do I feel that I can improve the communication I have with families?
- **How do I want the children to feel?** For example, do I want all the children to feel appreciated and supported? Do I want the children to feel free to investigate and make mistakes?

This book will help you consider and identify your values, goals, strengths, and weaknesses. Together, we will explore ways to use personal reflection to gain insight into creating the classroom you dream of having.

Reflection Is the Key

Most teachers would agree that conveying each child's worth in the classroom is an important goal; yet, not all teachers know how to follow through in making this happen. Having a vague sense that all children are worthy of being a part of the classroom community is not enough. Reflect on what it really means to value each child and then decide how to make that a reality. What do teachers do in a classroom that helps children get the message that they are valued and appreciated? Greeting each child upon entry to the classroom is one simple example. Looking for opportunities to check in with each child individually is another.

TEACHER: Lily, that is a fascinating picture with lots of bright colors! What is happening there?
LILY: This is my backyard with lots of flowers and a swing set.
TEACHER: I love backyards with flowers. Who plants and cares for them in your yard?
LILY: My mom does, and sometimes I help! I love the daisies. We bring them in the house and put them in a jar.
TEACHER: Sounds like fun. Where do you like to put them?

Simple check-ins such as this help establish and nurture attachments between the child and teacher and are important for turning into action the value of making each child feel worthy and important. Although many fine teachers do this intuitively, it is helpful to clarify your practices to ensure that the educational values actually are being communicated on a regular basis.

Sometimes, if a child is struggling or is challenging in some way, a teacher may feel that the child gets too much attention because the teacher has to make behavior interventions frequently. The teacher might avoid the very check-ins the child so desperately needs to keep the positive attachment going. If most interactions with a child are based on setting and enforcing limits, that attachment cannot flourish.

One of the obstacles that can get in the way of being an effective and reflective teacher is focusing on how to react to children's behavior. Often, teachers believe that if they have a strong repertoire of interventions, they can put a permanent end to specific types of misbehavior. Although having a broad repertoire of effective intervention strategies and good communication skills is necessary for excellence in teaching, managing young children's behavior and building a sense of community in classrooms has more to do with developing a philosophy, thinking about prevention, considering the organization and careful setup of the environment, and making a commitment to regularly examine how one's own behavior in the classroom affects the children.

Plan Ahead for Success

A reflective teacher must be honest with himself about his strengths and his weaknesses. Acknowledging where he has room for growth can be difficult. By recognizing and acknowledging his personal strengths and vulnerabilities, which everyone brings along with them into the classroom, a teacher can do the best possible job of responding appropriately to children and accessing support and consultation when necessary. And the additional bonus is that, through this kind of thoughtful teaching, the teacher becomes a better, stronger person!

Most early childhood teachers, for example, want an organized, peaceful classroom in which all the children are respectful of their classmates. Communicating these values, however, can be a real challenge. Consider the following.

Mrs. Langley, a teacher of four-year-olds, is frustrated with how her morning circle time activity is going. Maria, Sam, and Madison just cannot seem to keep their bodies to themselves, pay attention, or refrain from interrupting and disrupting the process. Mrs. Langley is tired of having to interrupt group time to remind these three to manage themselves and pay attention.

Trying to respond to each individual behavior is probably not the best plan, though it is a typical one. It would be more effective to think about how the children's challenging behaviors might be prevented in the first place. Planning ahead for success rather than reacting to failure takes patience and a willingness to acknowledge that the first impulse may not be the most effective one.

The teacher can take a number of approaches. Maybe the children need to sit near the teacher or the assistant during circle time. Perhaps they would do better sitting on chairs rather than on the rug. Perhaps one of the children could be the page turner during the story, thus giving the child something physically active to do. Perhaps the teacher could offer a child a fidget to manipulate during circle time. Rather than waiting for the children to misbehave and then thinking of something to do in response, plan a preventive intervention. Explain to each child what the plan will be at circle time and how it will be helpful.

Perhaps the teacher needs to step back from thinking individually about the three children and think about what might not be working in how she is organizing or managing circle time itself. If three or four children are having difficulties, the transition into circle time may be too long, and the early birds are already bored by the time the teacher actually begins the activity. Perhaps the stories are too long and detailed to read in a large group and hold everyone's attention, or the stories are too short or so familiar that they have begun to lose their appeal. Maybe the children need to do a music and movement experience at the beginning of circle time to get their wiggles out.

Stepping back and reflecting on one's own behavior and planning, rather than simply looking at what the children are doing, takes a willingness to admit that one's initial approach could be improved.

Communicate Values

At first glance, young children can appear extremely impulsive and unpredictable, as well as adorable and appealing. The adults charged with teaching them want to enable children to function optimally at school—to learn to interact with peers, to pay attention to teachers, to take turns, to cooperate in play, to learn specific pre-academic skills, and to experience joy in learning. What is not always obvious to educators is that, to support such optimal functioning, a very broad, holistic approach to teaching is required. The teacher must pay attention to what she is doing, how she is doing it, and why. If her approach is not bringing about the desired results, then the approach needs some re-evaluation.

Damian loves to play with LEGOs and wants to keep them all to himself. Each day, he goes over to the small-manipulatives table, takes out the bin of blocks, and begins to play. If other children come over, he becomes upset when they take any of the LEGOs out of the bin, worrying that they might use one that he "needs." Despite the fact that there are plenty of LEGOs available, he grabs the blocks from the other children and does not share.

Teachers want to teach children that cooperating with one another and sharing are values and expectations in the classroom. A teacher's first thoughts about Damian's behavior might be that he needs to learn how to share and that he cannot keep all of the LEGOs to himself. Therefore, a typical reaction and response may be, "Damian, in this classroom, all of the children can use the materials. You need to let the other children have some LEGOs, or you won't be able to continue to play with them." This response appears reasonable, since grabbing from others is unacceptable. However, if the teacher considers how to meet the child's apparent need to have lots of LEGOs, she is more likely to be successful in teaching the value of sharing.

Children are rarely pleased when they hear that they cannot do something. A different approach might look like this: "Damian, I see that it's hard for you when other children are using the LEGOs. What bothers you about Sammy using them?" Damian might respond that he might need the ones Sammy has. The teacher then can provide a tray or plastic bowl and put a large number of LEGOs in it. She can explain to Damian that those LEGOs are just for him; no one else can use them. If anyone wants to use other LEGOs, they must get them from the bin. Those are for sharing, but the ones in the tray or bowl are just for Damian.

Although it may seem that the teacher is not really teaching Damian to share, what is happening is that she is helping Damian tolerate sharing by enabling him to feel that he will have enough and therefore does not have to worry about needing what the others are using. This approach recognizes the purpose behind Damian's behavior, acknowledges his need, and reassures him that his need will be met.

Know Your Strengths and Weaknesses

It is a tall order, all of these skills that preschoolers need to gain before they go off to kindergarten! The early childhood educator's plate is quite full. It may feel like the best way to help children function well at school and gain these skills is to just jump in, develop some fun curriculum plans, and get going! However, while implementing curriculum and operating the classroom itself are essential, a significant amount of planning is required. In particular, take the time to reflect on which situations you find particularly challenging and which situations you feel that you handle pretty well.

Most teachers feel more competent dealing with some types of behaviors or personality styles and less confident in dealing with others. Knowing what these are will help teachers not only hone their skills, but also be more alert to how they respond to the behaviors they find especially challenging.

For example, some teachers are quite patient with the clingy child who has anxieties about separation. One teacher may be perfectly comfortable holding that child on her lap or keeping the child next to her as she moves about the classroom; another teacher may experience this same child very differently and may be frustrated by the clinginess. Similarly, in dealing with a defiant child, some teachers can be very inventive and creative, coming up with many ways of using humor to defuse the child's anger and obstinacy. Other teachers may view the defiance as an attack on their authority and will engage in a power struggle with the child. Consider the following example.

Samantha does not like to participate in clean-up time after free play. When the teacher tells the children that it is time to put toys away, Samantha puts her hands on her hips and loudly declares, "No way! You do it!"

A teacher who sees Samantha's defiance as a battle of wills may assert her authority. "Samantha, the rule in our classroom is that everyone helps with cleanup. If you choose not to help, you will have to sit on the porch when we go outside to play, and you won't be able to play for as many minutes if you don't help us now." Samantha is likely to react with further defiance. Both of them are now stuck, with neither wanting to give in. Frequently when a teacher threatens a particular consequence for a behavior, the child will go ahead and test to see if the teacher actually will follow through. Thus, the attempt to achieve compliance backfires, leaving both the child and the teacher frustrated and unhappy.

The teacher who is more comfortable with defiance may use humor to defuse the situation, saying, "Oh, my gosh! What a great idea! If I were an octopus and had eight arms, I could do all the cleanup myself! But look at me: I only have two arms, and that's not nearly enough. I need help! If you and I put away these toys together, we'll have four arms, and that's almost as much as an octopus. And, if we invite two more children to help, we'll have eight arms!" Humor might not work every time, but it works often. The teacher's enthusiasm when responding in this manner can go a long way toward engaging the child's cooperation.

Recognizing that a child is pushing one's buttons—and avoiding the customary response—is a skill that must be developed over time. Building insight through reflection means that, sometimes, the teacher will not handle a situation well. For example, a teacher who is feeling stressed, tired, or worried about personal concerns may respond insensitively to the children in her class. One of the wonderful advantages of being a teacher is that there are always opportunities to do a better job, to address mistakes, and to move forward more positively. Young children are developing the capacity to be reflective about their own behavior. They are fairly impulsive and often will lash out or behave inappropriately as a result of intense momentary feelings that overwhelm their self-control. The teacher can be a role model and demonstrate self-reflection through his willingness to acknowledge his mistakes.

Ms. Vargas is having a difficult day. She ran late this morning, spilled coffee on her blouse, and must juggle her schedule to take her son to the dentist in the afternoon.

For days, Ms. Vargas has been working on a papier-mâché project with the children. They are studying bodies of water to see how big the nearby ocean is in relation to the land. Phoebe, a boisterous and sometimes bossy four-year-old, comments that another child's globe looks really stupid and ugly.

Ms. Vargas yells, "Phoebe, you need to leave this table right now for using such unkind words! You should pay more attention to your own globe and not criticize others. Yours isn't so perfect, either!"

Phoebe skulks away from the table and scowls, feeling angry and hurt.

Everyone has a bad day once in a while. And when that happens, it is all too easy to say something hurtful. The good news is that when a teacher makes such a mistake, the teacher and the child both have an opportunity for growth. Later that evening, as Ms. Vargas reflects on her day, she may realize that her reaction was inappropriate, even though Phoebe's behavior also was unacceptable. The next day, she could sit down with Phoebe and talk about the situation:

> Phoebe, I was thinking about what happened yesterday afternoon at the art table when I yelled at you for saying unkind words to your friend. I was having a bad day and was feeling kind of crabby, and I shouldn't have yelled at you like that or talked about your globe in that way. That wasn't nice. There I was, angry at you for being unkind to

your friend, and then I was unkind to you! You do need to work on using kind words with your friends, and I need to work on not taking out my own crabbiness out on children at school if I'm having a bad day! I am really sorry I yelled at you like that. I hope you can forgive me.

In all but the rarest of cases, the child will accept the teacher's apology, and both child and teacher will feel much better. In this way, the teacher is modeling reflection and personal responsibility. She is demonstrating the understanding that people's words can hurt, and she is making amends. By including what Phoebe needs to work on, the teacher makes it clear that the child's behavior was unacceptable as well. It is very validating for children to experience an adult demonstrating remorse in this way. Some teachers might worry that perhaps it will make them appear weak. On the contrary, the teacher looks stronger because she is unafraid to acknowledge her own imperfections. The teacher is modeling her values of peaceful cooperation, responsibility, forgiveness, and respect. Reflective teachers help create reflective children.

Validate Children's Feelings

Working with young children exposes teachers to some of the intense developmental struggles of the first five years of life, including attachment, separation, autonomy, initiative, and beginning relationships with peers. Part of the process of learning to be a reflective teacher is to learn to accept children's feelings, even though their behavior must be limited at times. When a child experiences having her feelings validated, she is much more likely to cooperate with a limit that must be set.

Terri loves going through an obstacle course the teachers have set up outside, and she has no interest in coming inside for story time and lunch. She begins to scream that she will not go in. Instead of simply insisting that it is time to go, her teacher says, "You had such a great time on the obstacle course this morning, Terri! You were really good at it, and it was a lot of fun! It is so hard to stop when you're having fun. Having to stop makes children really mad sometimes. How about if you go through it one more time, and I will make sure you can be the first one to have a turn this afternoon."

Terri is not thrilled to stop, but she is pleased to have one more turn. As she approaches the end of the obstacle course, the teacher takes her hand, congratulates her for excellence in obstacle-course skills, and walks her toward the classroom before she can begin to resist.

By validating her feelings, allowing her a little extra time, and connecting with her while leading her inside, this teacher cleverly distracts Terri from becoming upset again and helps reassure her that her moments on the beloved obstacle course are not totally over.

The act of validating children's feelings, while continuing to expect compliance with guidelines and norms, is very powerful for children. Teachers understand clearly the necessity for a schedule; this understanding is rarely so clear for children. Therefore, explicitly recognizing their difficulty in complying with scheduling expectations is very helpful.

Gaining Powerful Insights

Another way teachers can use reflection to improve their effectiveness in the classroom is to use their own feelings diagnostically. This is a tool that child therapists learn when they engage in play therapy with young children. Frequently, a child will set up games or play situations that will evoke the same or similar feelings on the part of the therapist that the child also is struggling with. It is a way for the child to convey his worries or vulnerabilities nonverbally and mostly unconsciously.

Years ago, as a young therapist, I was working with a five-year-old boy who loved to organize structured games for us to play in our therapy sessions. But, he would constantly change the rules or change the game in ways that would ensure that I would lose. Of course, as a therapist, it should not have been my goal to try to win the games; yet, at times I actually found myself feeling frustrated that no matter how I played the game, I always ended up not only losing but also feeling stupid because I had played it "wrong."

When I shared these feelings, about which I was fairly embarrassed, with a consultant, he gave me an insight that has stayed with me for many years. He suggested that this child, by orchestrating the games in this way, was letting me know how he feels in his life. In some part of his life, he must feel out of control, stupid, and like a loser. And he was sharing this with me.

Because children often show us their feelings through behavior rather than verbally, it is especially helpful for teachers to find ways to understand what underlies difficult behaviors. Using oneself in this way can be very enlightening. A simple example of this dynamic might work with a child who constantly needs to be defiant so that she can feel in control. Such a child can easily make a teacher feel out of control, because the teacher's authority is constantly being questioned. By looking underneath the angry or frustrated feelings the teacher has in relation to this child, she can recognize that feeling of being out of control.

In many cases, such children are struggling somewhere in their lives, and their attempts to control the teacher are attempts to control their own lives. If a teacher can use her own feelings diagnostically, she will understand the child better and may be able to arrive at more effective strategies for intervention. This requires a willingness to be honest with oneself, but it can be a powerful tool. A teacher's own feelings, even negative ones, are acceptable and can be dealt with in a way that does not harm children. By being honest with herself and seeking support from colleagues, a teacher can find positive ways to support the children with whom she works.

Frequently, teachers feel it is somehow unprofessional to feel anger toward a child. As a result, too often teachers do not acknowledge their negative feelings, maybe even deny that those feelings are there, but then act out those feelings in the classroom. Therefore, it is much better for teachers to acknowledge and accept their feelings toward the children they are teaching. Then, they can get the help and support to work through their feelings in a healthy, productive way.

Developing a Reflective Mindset

Being a reflective teacher opens up opportunities for growth, insight, and achieving excellence in one's work with children. How to get there? Take the time to look at interactions with children as a two-way street, examining both the child's behavior and your own response. Think about how the day went. What worked, and what did not? Analysis and reflection will help guide you to creating more good days in the future. Choose to look at each day in the classroom as a new opportunity to re-create the great days in new ways or to prevent some of the bad ones by changing one's approach. Getting there is not magic, but the results can be magical!

Questions for Reflection

This chapter describes the importance of being personally reflective to be an insightful teacher. Knowing one's personal and teaching strengths, as well as one's challenges and hot-button issues, enables a teacher to respond more professionally and more supportively to children.

This exercise is designed to help teachers think about themselves as teachers, identify their strengths and vulnerabilities, and choose one or two areas to focus on for growth.

1. Describe at least three areas of teaching that represent strengths for you and of which you feel proud.
2. Identify at least two areas of teaching that are especially challenging for you.
3. Identify three typical child behaviors that you feel especially comfortable and competent in handling—for example, separation feelings or defiance.
4. Identify at least two behaviors in children that you are acutely sensitive to, especially dislike, or may occasionally overreact to because of your strong feelings about them.
5. Choose at least one area of your teaching or one type of behavior in children that is difficult for you. Commit to working on this area during the next several months.
6. Make an initial plan for steps you can take to make progress in this area.
7. Consider your goals and values for your classroom. Write them down and keep the list handy as we move through the book. Refer to them often, adding and changing them as you feel appropriate.

Defining
Developmentally Appropriate
Expectations

Sometimes teachers' eyes glaze over when they hear the term *child development*. It may seem like an academic term with little bearing on what actually happens in classrooms every day. Actually, child development is very helpful, and here's why: Understanding which skills, abilities, interests, and emotional needs develop within certain age periods enables teachers to organize their classrooms and teaching approaches to support children. How does this work? All aspects of planning, including the physical setup of the classroom environment, curriculum development and implementation, communication with children, and behavioral guidelines and expectations, should arise out of an understanding of what is going on in the minds and bodies of the young children who will occupy that classroom. When an understanding of child development does not inform planning, the stage is set for significant amounts of misbehavior and the perceived need for lots of consequences.

Child Development:
Birth through Age Five

In this book, the framework for examining early developmental phases is the one used by Erik Erikson, one of the great psychological researchers of the mid-twentieth century. Erikson's developmental framework is divided into eight phases, each associated with an age period and each composed of a specific developmental challenge or "crisis" that a person must successfully resolve to move forward in a healthy, positive, productive way. Resolution of each developmental crisis does not need to be perfect, because all of us have incompletely resolved developmental issues as we move through life. Life provides children and adults with many opportunities to rework and resolve old conflicts.

What is needed is for a child to experience what psychoanalyst Donald Winnicott refers to as "the holding environment." One does not have to be the perfect parent or caregiver; one merely needs to be responsive to the developing child's needs most of the time. In doing so, the child experiences being held, in an emotional sense, and feeling secure. For an infant, the holding environment actually involves a great deal of physical holding, but Winnicott also means the term in a nonphysical sense: protecting, supporting, being emotionally attuned and close to the child, meeting physical and emotional needs. As a parent and as a professional working with young children, I have found Winnicott's perspective comforting! What a relief to know that my mistakes would not necessarily lead to a detrimental outcome for my children or my clients. The overall commitment to and follow-through with meeting children's needs is critical.

Keep in mind that children learn through exploration, interactions, trial and error, and with the help of supportive adults. The focus or goal of teachers should not be for children to learn through subtraction: deprivation, consequences, or punishment. Old notions of teaching someone a lesson by having that person suffer in some way as a result of wrongdoing are not helpful or productive. Often, when children suffer or experience consequences, they feel shame, humiliation, and resentment. This does not mean that setting boundaries and occasionally incorporating logical consequences into a response are unnecessary; however, seek other approaches and strategies first. Children express their needs through their behavior, and it is the adult's job to learn to understand the child's needs and to respond appropriately. When this happens, much inappropriate behavior can be avoided, prevented, or ameliorated.

Erik Erikson's Eight Stages of Psychological Development

Age Range	Developmental Task
0–1 year	Trust vs. Mistrust
1–3 years	Autonomy vs. Shame and Doubt
3–6 years	Initiative vs. Guilt
6–12 years	Industry vs. Inferiority
12–18 years	Identity vs. Role Confusion
18–35 years	Intimacy vs. Isolation
35–60 years	Generativity vs. Stagnation
60 years–End of Life	Integrity vs. Despair

Birth to Age One: Trust vs. Mistrust

During the first year of life, the groundwork is laid for healthy emotional functioning. The parent or caregiver must be responsive to the infant's needs most of the time. As a matter of fact, a child gradually learns to become independent through having his needs met. It is through the repeated experience of being responded to when in distress—being fed when hungry, changed when wet, held when uncomfortable, responded to when in need of human contact—that infants begin to develop trust and a deep sense that the world is an inviting place. Luckily for the sleep-deprived adults who care for them, babies arrive with lots of capacity to draw us into physical closeness with them. The softness of their little heads, the tenderness of their skin, even their smell stimulate a strong desire to hold and connect with them.

As babies begin to develop some self-soothing skills, such as sucking a thumb, finding a more comfortable physical position, playing with a mobile, and exploring their own bodies, parents and caregivers can hesitate a bit before picking the baby up when she whimpers. T. Berry Brazelton, highly regarded pediatrician and author of many books about parenting infants and toddlers, addresses the need for babies to develop self-soothing techniques. Although it is detrimental to young infants to leave them screaming in their cribs all alone, older infants benefit from having a little time to figure out how to calm themselves when they experience distress. The caregiver must use judgment, a sense of timing, sensitivity, and emotional attunement to assess the infant's state of need and then must respond accordingly.

The good news is that it is practically impossible for parents or caregivers to soothe a child each time she whimpers. As a result, babies will have many opportunities to begin to develop these self-soothing skills as they move through the first year of life.

For most babies, a balance is struck between the caregivers responding to the baby's needs and the baby beginning to develop some emerging ability to wait. As long as the balance is weighted heavily toward responsiveness, the baby moves into the second year with a feeling of safety and trust that she will be cared for. This trust enables the toddler to move into the next phase with the energy and confidence to explore the environment more autonomously.

So, what does a one-year-old who has mastered this phase look like? Such a child has a happy expression on her face much of the time; is interested and engaged in finding and exploring objects in the environment; wants to move around and engage with materials on her own; and delights in interaction with parents, caregivers, and other trusted adults. A one-year-old who has not experienced a good balance of having her needs met may look less happy, may have less interest in getting around and exploring materials in the environment, and may be more anxious about where the caregiving adults are. The sense of exhilaration in exploring the world may be muted or absent, and the child may be crabby or may become upset very easily and need a great deal of soothing and reassurance. All children will occasionally be upset and will need soothing; how much time is spent experiencing this need can indicate a less successful resolution of the task of the first year.

Following the principle that young children gradually develop the ability to be independent by having their dependency needs met, if a child appears less excited and content entering into his second year, he will need a great deal of reassurance and comfort from his parent or caregiver. He will need opportunities to explore on his own, but with lots of support to help him along the way. While some children appear not to care where the adults are as they run around the room and find toys to play with, others may need to keep the adult within sight or even close by to feel safe with such exploration. The more the adult is able to provide that support and physical presence, the more likely it is that the little one will develop the confidence to explore on his own. With very young children, the "sink or swim" approach is rarely effective. Their ability to move away on their own is connected to their sense of security and safety arising out of a trusting relationship with a dependable and emotionally available adult.

Note: When attempting to understand what may underlie a child's apparent unhappiness or difficult temperament, rule out any physical causes first. A child with allergies or a chronic medical condition is sure to be less content than a truly healthy one. A pediatrician should assess a little one's overall health to rule out any physical issues.

Age One to Age Three: Autonomy vs. Shame and Doubt

The word *autonomy* means "the freedom from control or external influence; independence." Although the drive for autonomy begins during this phase, issues related to one's freedom and control can last throughout life. Thinking about toddlers, you may be struck by what an amazing, delightful, yet challenging period of development this is! So much is going on in those little brains, bodies, and spirits during this time. It is hard to keep up with toddlers, physically and in every other way. The two most obvious changes in toddlers are in the areas of physical mobility and language development.

Exploration

What adult has not giggled at a toddler's headlong rush into the larger world? It is such a joy to observe the unbridled enthusiasm and wonder with which toddlers embrace exploration. On one hand, parents or caregivers may feel relieved that their little ones are now capable of moving about on their own, needing to be held and carried less. To some extent, this frees up the adults to attend to various tasks of daily life that were a challenge when they needed to be holding an infant much of the time. On the other hand, toddlers' explorations must be closely monitored to ensure their safety. Figuring out the balance between this newfound independence and the necessary monitoring can be challenging.

When children are able to freely explore their environments, life is exciting, and new discoveries lie around every corner. Dangers lurk as well, and adults must be constantly on the lookout to provide protection. This protection sometimes must take the form of limits, and the adult begins to say no to the child. During this phase of development, sensitive parents and caregivers should reflect on the child's development and temperament and organize the environment in ways that prevent the need for constant limits, removing dangerous or delicate objects from the reach of little hands. Especially in classrooms, the caregiver must give careful thought to the arrangement of toys and materials, so that many interesting things will be available for the child to explore on his own without adult intervention.

Erikson's concepts of shame and doubt refer to the possibility that a young child who is constantly limited in his explorations might begin to feel that there is something wrong with him. Exploration is a natural drive at this age. It is hardwired into our brains to seek new experiences and master physical challenges. If adults frequently become angry or irritated and limit such exploration, the child might feel that something about him is not acceptable. The goal during this phase is to provide an environment rich in stimulation and materials to explore with as few dangers as possible. Understanding that toddlers must check out whatever is around them will help the adults reflect on and organize the environment in ways that minimize conflict and the need for limits.

Two-year-old Olivia has gotten into the habit of reaching up over her head to attempt to grab paper from a high shelf, instead of taking paper kept on a lower shelf for the children's use. Sometimes she becomes quite upset when she cannot reach the paper on the high shelf, and she screams in frustration. The teacher has shown her many times that paper is available for her on a lower shelf.

One day, as Olivia is once again reaching for the paper on the higher shelf, the teacher calls out, "Olivia, I just saw some pink paper waiting for you on the shelf by your knees! I bet you can grab it before I can count to three!" Olivia looks at her teacher, then quickly finds the pink paper on her own, smiling proudly.

The teacher's understanding of Olivia's wish for autonomy helped her to find a solution to Olivia's frustration. If the teacher had responded by reminding Olivia of the rule or by removing her from the area, she would have increased Olivia's frustration. In many cases, understanding the reason for a child's behavior and being creative in redirecting her is effective.

Most teachers are familiar with the term *the terrible twos* and have experienced its meaning firsthand. While not all two-year-olds have extreme autonomy struggles, it is quite common for children between the ages of two and three to become quite firmly attached to what they want and to assert themselves fiercely when crossed. "No, I won't!" or

"No! Mine!" are common expressions among this crowd. Teachers of two-year-olds must plan carefully to avoid situations in which they make direct commands; they must be very creative in how they communicate expectations in the classroom.

One of the messages I frequently give to early childhood educators in workshops relates to young children's developmental "job." When teachers complain about controlling, challenging, or defiant young children, I attempt to reframe this behavior by explaining that, in a way, this is part of the child's job. Young children are in the business of exploring their world. They see that they are smaller and less powerful than adults; yet, they want to have as much control over their experiences as possible. Therefore, it is their developmental job to push the limits, to see how far they can go, to find out how much control they can have. At the same time, we must remember what constitutes our job: providing young children the opportunities they need to explore safely, to begin to make choices, and to have some power over themselves within clear limits and safe boundaries. It is actually quite frightening for young children to not experience safe boundaries and limits to their explorations and demands. Although they may fight against these limits, when presented in a reasonable, caring, yet firm way, limits are deeply comforting.

Understanding the two-year-old's need to feel in control of himself in a big, grownup world will enable teachers to find ways of engaging cooperation without confrontations. "As soon as the toys are put away, we're going to go outside to play!" is a much wiser comment than, "If you don't put the toys away, we can't go out to play!" Finding ways of gaining compliance through understanding what motivates young children and capturing their interests and will go a long way toward maintaining peaceful toddler classrooms.

Language Development

Sometimes, as toddlers develop more language skills, adults may become confused about setting limits. For young children, receptive language develops first; a young child understands many more words or phrases than he can say. Expressive language, the words and phrases the child is able to say, develops a bit later.

It is often a joy for parents and caregivers to say to a toddler, "Go get your baby doll! Let's put on her clothes!" and see the little one go right over to the toy shelf and bring the baby doll and her dress to the caregiver. However, this recognition of the young child's developing receptive language skills can lead adults to have unrealistic expectations. Many an adult has insisted, in expressing his frustration with the young child's perceived disobedience, "But he knows perfectly well what *no* means!" This may be true, but there is frequently a vast distance between cognitively understanding what the word *no* means and actually having enough self-control to stop an action. This is why adults must continue to use physical intervention and distraction to set limits with toddlers, even well beyond the time when the children understand the meanings of the adults' words.

Through the repeated experience of being gently physically stopped, the child develops the ability to stop herself. Calling out, "No!" from across the room and then getting aggravated that the toddler continues to play in the dirt surrounding the houseplant is not an appropriate response. Instead, it is better to get up and go over to the child and explain, "The plant's dirt is not for playing. Let's get you a bin of sand to play with!" Then the adult can take the child by the hand and lead her away from the houseplant. Recognizing that this kind of response is required for the toddler to remain safe while she learns appropriate exploration behavior will help adults feel less stressed and frustrated when toddlers seem to be ignoring them.

Mark heads over to the puzzle table only to find that Theo is working on the puzzle he planned to use. The teacher knows that Mark loves horses and that there is another horse puzzle in the puzzle rack. She kneels down and says, "Mark, Theo is doing that horse puzzle right now, but I know you love the one with the purple horse. That puzzle is in the rack waiting just for you! See if you can find it!"

The teacher's physical proximity and redirection help to reduce the likelihood that this emerging conflict between the children will progress to pushing, grabbing, or shoving—common behaviors at this age.

Separation

Another developmental task for toddlers is learning to manage their feelings about separation from their parents if they are cared for regularly by child care providers. Although infants also experience feelings of separation from their parents, the responsibility for supporting them lies with the adults who care for them. Infants do not yet have the necessary language or motor skills to work through such feelings on their own. Comforting and consistent goodbye routines are essential to help ease the transition. Solid communication between home and child care provider is critical for maintaining patterns of caregiving that make sense to the child and provide continuity between home and child care.

As infants move into toddlerhood and can explore their environment more independently, they often express their feelings about separation through their emerging language and their behaviors. This is the period in which many young children develop attachments to transitional objects or "lovies," beloved toys or blankets that symbolize their attachment to their family. For many toddlers, having such objects with them helps them to feel secure. Often a toddler will need his lovie to go to sleep at nap time or to hold while he transitions into the classroom in the morning. This can present a challenge to program staff, who may be understandably concerned about how to keep these objects safe and not lose track of them.

Because of such concerns, sometimes child care programs develop rules restricting the use of such transitional objects. Some do not allow children to bring them at all; others require children to keep their lovies in their backpacks or their cubbies while they are in the classroom. Such rules represent attempts to maintain order, but, unfortunately, that order is achieved at the expense of meeting young children's emotional needs. Because a transitional object represents the child's sense of comfort and security, not allowing the child access to it sends the message that the child's need for security is not important. When considered through the lens of child development, transitional objects should be welcomed at school, and staff must make an effort to ensure that these objects will not be lost or damaged. A common strategy for accomplishing this may include allowing a child to hold the lovie until he is ready to play with toys in the classroom, at which time he can place his lovie in his cubby. If a child feels needy during the day, he should feel free to go and get his lovie.

Sometimes a special soft chair or perhaps the cozy reading area with large pillows and books can be the spot where the child can hold and cuddle his transitional object, emotionally refueling himself so that he can continue his day.

At the beginning of a program, when young children are just starting to come to a child care center, it is hugely helpful if staff allow those who are especially attached to their transitional objects to carry them around for a period of time, perhaps the first week or two. This demands a great deal of attention and supervision from caregivers, but the sense of comfort and security it provides is well worth the effort. Young children adjust much more easily to the child care environment when they can keep their sense of comfort with them!

Understanding the psychological meaning of a child's wish for his transitional object can help teachers have more appropriate expectations for the child and provide the necessary supports for the child to function more successfully. Taking the extra time to think about these needs and to plan for them ends up making caregivers' lives easier, because the children feel more secure and welcome and thus are less likely to engage in negative behaviors.

Ayisha is two years old and has been in a full-day child care program for one year. She has grown attached to a particular doll in the housekeeping area. Each morning when she arrives, she goes to find "her" doll, picks it up, and carries it around with her for much of the morning. One day she arrives a bit later than usual, and another child has chosen to play with the doll. Ayisha marches right over to the child and grabs the doll, shouting, "Mine!"

The caregiver has some choices in responding to this situation. Focusing on the communality of classroom materials, she could take the position that this is an opportunity to insist on sharing. She could point out that all of the dolls are available to anyone who would like to play with them, possibly offering Ayisha a different doll. Most likely, that will not satisfy Ayisha, and she will protest loudly.

Another choice could be to explain to Susie that the doll she chose is Ayisha's favorite doll, and it helps her settle down when she arrives in the morning. However, it is not Susie's fault that she chose the doll that was lying in the crib in the housekeeping area. It is not fair to ask her to give the doll to Ayisha.

Knowing that Ayisha needs to play with that particular doll in the morning, it would be a better idea for the caregiver to put the doll aside for Ayisha. Perhaps that doll could be set in Ayisha's cubby or kept on a high shelf. Ayisha could ask for it if she wants it, and other children will not be able to take it, thus avoiding a predictable conflict.

Individualizing within a program to meet a child's needs is a strategy for success, and the keys to successful individualization are reflection, thought, and planning on the part of the caregiver. While it is true that toys and dolls are available for any child to use, if an individual child develops a special attachment to a toy that seems to help the child comfortably function in the child care environment, then making an exception to the general expectation makes sense. This is especially true in a toddler classroom, where children are more limited in their ability to talk through their feelings about separation. Usually these attachments to materials within classrooms do not last for long, and it is likely that Ayisha soon will not need to hold this doll each morning.

When teachers understand the developmental phase that children are experiencing and view their behaviors within the context of that phase, they have an opportunity to respond more sensitively to children and help them function better. This requires a willingness to reflect on the meaning of behaviors. As toddlers continue to grow and develop, their ability to stop themselves gradually emerges. Two-year-olds continue to need a great deal of physical intervention by their parents and caregivers, but they also can respond to verbal reminders at times, especially if the issue involved is not one in which they are hugely invested.

Sharing (or Not)

It is natural and typical for toddlers to be very territorial and not terribly receptive to the idea of sharing. Preventive measures such as providing individual trays or containers for play materials can meet toddlers' needs to have their own stuff while providing ample supplies to everyone. Keep the focus on the goal of successful functioning in the classroom, in which each child has equal access to play materials and can play productively without interfering with anyone else. The developmental goal at this age is productive play, not understanding the concept of sharing. Learning to share is a long-term goal.

Short Attention Span

One of the most challenging aspects of teaching toddlers is their naturally short attention spans, which require caregivers to have lots of different activities ready each day. Even if the children enjoy the art materials the teacher has laid out, they are not likely to stay with that exploration for longer than ten minutes. The same is true for other activities throughout the classroom. Therefore, teachers of toddlers have to be really good at keeping simple yet engaging explorations available and accessible for the children.

A horde of toddlers is gathered in and around the climber in the classroom. There's a lot of pushing and shoving and general unhappiness among the children. Thinking quickly, the teacher brings out some different materials to engage the children in gross motor play: a cloth tunnel for crawling through, an obstacle course created with large wooden blocks, and a long strip of masking tape on the rug. The children around the climber begin to move away to explore the new materials.

Build a long list of quick and easy ideas for little ones. To keep interest high, limit the available materials in any given center, and rotate new materials into the centers frequently. Young children are highly responsive to their teachers' enthusiasm, so practically any new material will be extremely compelling to them if it is presented with zest! Whether it is a new storybook, a song, a movement activity, or a new paint color, little ones will respond quite well to the teacher's enthusiastic presentation of this new option for productive play.

Age Three to Age Five: Initiative vs. Guilt

Erikson saw children in the preschool years as moving increasingly out into the wider world beyond home and family. During this period, children meet lots of new peers and adults, begin to develop real friendships, and are primed for learning many new skills, including the academic skills that will prepare them for elementary school. As children develop more sophisticated thinking and language skills, they come up with more ideas about what they want to do and how they want to do it. Consequently, opportunities arise for them to make decisions and engage in behaviors that will meet with adult disapproval.

Testing the boundaries of their freedom is important for preschoolers. Erikson saw this period as a time for children to develop their sense of initiative and their confidence in their ability to carry out ideas and impact their environment. At the same time, when their ideas and behaviors meet with disapproval from adults whom they love and respect, they must begin to learn to reflect on their own choices and sometimes make changes. This process of reflection can lead to feelings of guilt over having done something wrong and remorse or regret for inappropriate behavior.

The term *self-regulation* has become a buzzword in educational circles in recent years. It refers to the ability of a child to manage, modulate, and regulate her feelings and behavior. The child who is able to listen to and follow through on directions, to follow group expectations and norms, and to negotiate conflict with peers and engage in problem solving is said to have good self-regulation skills. Research shows that such skills are actually more predictive of later school success than academic skills such as knowing letters and numbers, beginning word recognition, and so on. If a child has the academic skills but is not able to attend to the teacher, easily follow classroom guidelines, or problem solve with peers, then academic knowledge is not likely to be as useful to her. It is the ability to make use of one's knowledge in the context of strong social-emotional skills that ensures school success.

Part of what enables young children to develop the self-regulation skills is the ability—and opportunity—to reflect on their behavior. Children need to understand that hurting others' feelings or not following classroom safety guidelines has a negative impact; recognizing this may at times lead to some sense of remorse or guilt. This is a good thing, as it represents the beginning of a conscience, the ability to discern right from wrong and to make moral choices.

The prefrontal cortex in the brain helps us think through decisions about behavior and make good choices for ourselves. This part of the brain is not highly developed in young children; that is why they are impulsive and act on feelings quickly without thinking through the impact of their behavior. Good teaching can help children as they develop this capacity during the preschool years. The psychological goal for this period is to achieve a strong capacity for initiative and a limited amount of guilt. The ways teachers provide limits and boundaries in the classroom and help children solve problems will determine whether the children experience initiative or are burdened with guilt.

Erikson developed his theory during a time when it was common for adults to be quite harsh with children, when childrearing focused on setting high expectations for behavioral compliance. There was little room for accepting the boisterous and mischievous behaviors common in young children who are figuring out their world and how much control they can have over their experiences.

Today's society is quite different from Erikson's. Many families are struggling economically, working multiple jobs, and needing a variety of child care arrangements for their young children. In these families, life can feel unpredictable for the children, who experience multiple transitions within their day and are cared for by many different adults who may have different styles of managing behavior. Because of the many demands on parents, they may not have the energy and time to invest in supportively and patiently teaching appropriate behavior and providing a proper balance between the need for compliance and the need for freedom to explore within a safe, supervised setting. Some children face extreme situations, such as being left unsupervised for significant amounts of time and needing to figure out on their own how to behave and interact with others. At other times, children may face firm demands for compliance from their parents or other caregivers who are engaged in daily tasks that are not suited to engaging young children's interests. Sometimes families react to busy schedules and limited time with children by indulging the children and resisting setting limits. When children do not experience consistent, developmentally appropriate expectations, they are likely to have difficulty in balancing safe exploration and appropriate compliance. These children may not know how to organize themselves to move through a classroom and engage with other children and materials in productive ways.

Learning about a child's home environment and daily routine is essential for teachers to develop appropriate expectations for such children. Remember that each child's situation is different, and the fact that a parent works more than one job or the child has more than one caregiver during the day does not automatically mean the child will suffer. Many families do an excellent job of raising their children despite all kinds of challenges in their lives. Learn about the child through his behaviors in the classroom, by getting to know the family, and by learning about their home life. Then, create a plan for helping that child learn the necessary skills to succeed in the classroom.

Defiance

Often, teachers complain about children who neither seem to feel any remorse nor exhibit an ability to reflect on their behavior. These children are defiant, staking their ground and sticking with it, acting uninterested in the teacher's attempts to set limits or help them see that their actions at times are inappropriate or hurtful to others. Frequently teachers will say that the parents are not providing appropriate limits at home and, consequently, are causing difficulties in the classroom setting when the children refuse to go along with group expectations.

Consider that perhaps parents do not understand how children develop self-esteem and they fear that setting limits will damage a child's confidence and sense of self. Children need a balance between freedom to explore, initiate, and impact their environments, and having safe limits and boundaries provided by their families. This can certainly be a frustrating challenge for teachers, but they must keep in mind that they can control only what they do in their classrooms. Their main focus and much of their energy needs to be directed at understanding and planning for the children's needs within the classroom setting.

Aidan is a four-year-old child who has a hard time saying yes. Much of the time, he defies the teacher's requests in the classroom, refusing to go along with a variety of guidelines and apparently unconcerned about how others feel when he insists on getting his way.

At clean-up time, he wanders around the room instead of participating. When it is time to come to the rug for the daily classroom stories and meeting time, he dallies somewhere in the classroom. If a child is sitting where Aidan wants to sit at snack time, he will loudly insist on getting the other child's seat. When he plays basketball during outdoor time, he refuses to allow others to have a turn to shoot a basket. When the teacher intervenes, Aidan appears not to be bothered and insists on having his way.

How can the teacher help Aidan develop the ability to care about the impact of his behavior on his classmates? This is a long-term proposition. Remembering that young children's prefrontal cortexes are just developing the ability to think about what they do and to plan appropriate actions, the teacher must develop a specific approach for Aidan that involves some preventive intervention strategies as well as responses that do not allow him to take advantage of others. While not demanding that he demonstrate actual concern for others' feelings, she can limit his behavior.

For example, in regard to the basketball issue, the teacher can stay with the children to monitor and create opportunities for every child to have a turn to take shots at the basket. For Aidan, it might be helpful to give him a certain number of turns in a row before he must let someone else have a go. During someone else's turn, he could have another task to do, such as learning to dribble or playing catch with the teacher while he waits for his next turn at the basket.

At snack time, she could discuss with Aidan ahead of time where he would like to sit, possibly even assigning him a regular seat next to the teacher. Knowing that Aidan has difficulties making good choices for himself will enable the teacher to take preventive action to help Aidan be successful in the classroom setting.

Once some of Aidan's inappropriate behavior patterns are successfully addressed, over time the teacher can share with him how others feel when he is hurtful or inconsiderate. Asking a child to look at his peer's face and see the expression on it can be helpful in this process. "Do you see how Jonathan looks right now? He is feeling sad." Even if Aidan appears unconcerned, recognizing that his behavior has had an impact on someone else is the first step toward developing the ability to be reflective. The teacher may want to add a comment such as, "You might be able to think of something that could help Jonathan feel better. If you think of anything, I'm sure Jonathan would be pleased." Including the word *might* allows Aidan a choice, which empowers him.

When an adult insists that a child care about how a peer feels in response to something hurtful that the child has done, the child often will become defensive or unresponsive. When the teacher shows the child his peer's feelings without insisting that the child do something to address them, the child is more likely to begin to care. Children do not like to be confronted or forced to behave in certain ways. They want to feel like they have some control. When teachers suggest—but do not insist—that children do something caring for a peer, they are much more likely to make the choice to do so. It would be easy to respond to each of Aidan's inappropriate behaviors with some kind of limit or an expression of the teacher's frustration or disapproval. While Aidan does need to be prevented from hurting others, it is equally important for the teacher to think about the underlying reasons for Aidan's actions and to arrive at strategies that will enable him to need fewer interventions. This kind of planning ahead for success requires reflection and consideration on the part of the teacher, but it helps both teacher and child by preventing such defiant disruptions and creating a more smoothly running classroom.

Cooperative Play

One of the major areas of development during the preschool period is cooperative play skills. Young toddlers tend to engage in parallel play, using similar materials in close proximity to but not necessarily engaged with another child. Between ages two and three, children often begin to engage in associative play, in which they play with similar materials in close proximity to one another and make brief comments to one another that may relate to what they are doing or playing with. During the preschool years, children usually move from associative play into cooperative play, in which they discuss and plan their play together, cooperate in how they will use the materials, and negotiate roles in fantasy play.

Learning how to plan and execute ideas about what to play with and how the play will proceed is often not a smooth process. There are often disagreements and conflicts to resolve along the road to productive cooperative play. Understanding that this important developmental path is a rocky one will help teachers have reasonable expectations and respond to children's conflicts with caring and support rather than frustration and impatience.

Four-year-old Courtney loves to play in the housekeeping area, and she has clear ideas about role assignments for fantasy play there. One day, David and Elliott decide to make the housekeeping area into a firehouse. While they are busy cleaning their hoses and making sure they have their helmets ready in case they are called to a fire, Courtney comes over and wants to play at cooking and serving lunch for her pretend family.

The boys immediately protest, insisting that this is not someone's house but the firehouse where the firefighters stay when they are at work. Courtney is having none of that. A loud argument ensues, and Courtney yells, "No! This is my kitchen! It's not for firemen! You can play over there!" The boys stand their ground, refusing to leave.

Knowing that the children are learning how to problem solve, the teacher listens to the children's explanations of the situation and offers a potential solution: "How about if Courtney is the cook at the firehouse, and she makes lunch for the firefighters? That way, you all can play here." The boys question whether a girl can be in a firehouse, but when the teacher assures them that women can be and are firefighters, too, they relent. Courtney is ambivalent about not being a mom in her family's kitchen, but the enthusiasm of the boys' play and her determination to be the cook wins the day.

Of course, this play situation could have been resolved in a number of different ways. What is significant is the teacher's focus on ensuring that all of the children who want to engage in fantasy play can do so. The teacher models how to compromise and expand the play. Had the teacher decided that since the boys arrived first Courtney needed to find something else to do, or had she sent the boys and Courtney away from the housekeeping area altogether because they were not working out the conflict, the children would have missed an opportunity to learn valuable play skills. Because of her understanding that preschoolers often need help in developing their cooperative play skills, the teacher could provide just that.

Some children are less adept at interactive play than others. Teachers often worry about the child who tends to play by herself and does not seem comfortable approaching other children to enter into play. For some children, this wish to engage in solitary play may be developmentally appropriate. If a three-year-old tends to play by herself, it is not necessary for the teacher to push interactional play unless the child seems unhappy or isolated. Some children have extremely active imaginations and enjoy creating play experiences in which they are the only actor and can carry out exactly the plans they have in their heads.

The ability to compromise and negotiate with others regarding play comes more easily to some children than others and is not automatically a sign of a developmental problem. A reasonable goal for preschoolers is that, by the time they are in their prekindergarten year, they will begin to have some experiences of successful play with others at school.

View the child holistically: Does the child seem happy at school? Is she frequently looking at groups of children who are playing together and appearing sad or intimidated? Does the child engage with materials appropriately and experience a sense of competence and confidence in her play activities? As a child moves into her prekindergarten year, if she still tends to play by herself most of the time, it may be a good idea to think of ways to create experiences for her to play with others occasionally. Teachers can do this by considering who shares interests with the child—for example, inviting another child to do puzzles with the child who loves challenging puzzles. A teacher could have a day in which he pairs play partners for certain activity periods, assigning the partners based on his understanding of who might work and play well with whom. This approach also can be useful in attempting to interrupt partnerships that are not so productive, such as buddies who want to play together much of the time but end up spending a lot of their time squabbling.

Teachers can facilitate meaningful play by introducing children to new interactional play experiences with peers and by helping children move beyond unproductive play partnerships. Productive cooperative play creates new learning opportunities, cognitively as well as socially.

Sharing

Sharing seems to represent a core value for many preschool teachers. It is necessary for young children to learn how to cooperate in the use of classroom materials; however, sharing often involves giving up what one has so that someone else can have it, and this is very difficult for young children. Children become attached to things they invest themselves in, whether it be toys, materials, ideas for play, or being the first in line. Sharing is challenging and something that is learned slowly.

Some children seem to have an easier time with sharing than others, but the child who is more possessive is not being bad or difficult. Wanting to keep the teacher's attention or to play with the favored red fire truck is normal on the part of children, and their feelings should be treated as such.

Charlie enjoys playing with the yellow dump truck in the block area. Every day during free-choice time, he heads straight to the truck and plays with it until time to eat lunch. One day, Grace arrives in the block center and wants to play with the yellow dump truck. Charlie howls in protest.

One early childhood program found a solution to this type of problem that worked extremely well. Because I worked at this program for many years, I was able to watch the policy in action over a long period of time, and it never lost its effectiveness. If a child chose something to play with in the classroom, he could keep it as long as he wanted, even if he played with it during the entire free-choice time. If he needed to go to the bathroom and was not finished playing with the toy, he could ask the teacher to watch it for him so that no one else could play with it. However, if a child left a toy or play material to go to another part of the room and do something else, then the toy or material was open for anyone else to play with.

When one child wanted to play with a toy that someone else was using, the teacher would explain, "Grace, Charlie is using that now. Let's ask him to give it to you when he is finished." The teacher would help Grace let Charlie know that she wanted to use it as soon as Charlie was finished. Initially, when the children were just becoming familiar with this policy, the teacher would ask Charlie, "Grace would like a turn with that truck. As soon as you're finished with it, will you be sure and give it to her?" Sometimes, when a child or a teacher asked that question, the child who was playing with the toy would simply hand it over right on the spot. However, it was perfectly fine for Charlie to keep the truck as long as he wanted to play with it. The task then was for the teacher to help Grace find something else to play with while she waited for the truck.

Obviously, it is important to have multiples of vehicles or special toys in the classroom whenever possible. Bringing in one gorgeous, new yellow dump truck when there are no other yellow dump trucks in the classroom may be asking for trouble. Provide ample supplies of appealing play materials to reduce the need for children to give up what they are playing with or for the teacher to ask children repeatedly to wait for a turn.

Of course, it is not acceptable for a child to hoard a toy or material simply to lord it over another child or to tease another child by saying, "Ha, ha! I can keep this as long as I want, and you can't have it!" But, when children have permission to hold on to their toys and materials for as long as they want to use them, they are much less likely to grab or tease others about it. When children know they can have what they need, they actually tend to be more generous, because they know the decision to let go of what they are using is theirs to make.

In certain situations, it may be necessary to limit turns with play materials, such as on the swings outside. In those situations, the teacher can create a list of the children who want a turn, and each child can use the play material for a limited period of time. The time allotted, however, should not be extremely short just to assure every child of a turn.

Occasionally, a child who is on the list may not end up getting a turn that day because so many children want a turn. In those rare instances, that child would be the first to have a turn the next morning.

Recognize that, merely by being in a group preschool setting, children already are sharing quite a lot. They share the space, the materials, and the adults' attention. Sharing all of these things is challenging for young children! By understanding the complexities involved in the experience of sharing, teachers can have age-appropriate expectations in this regard and can develop policies that support young children's needs and result in more positive behaviors in the classroom.

Understanding the primary developmental tasks of the first five years of life, as well as the specific challenges presented by early experiences in group settings, enables teachers to have reasonable, age-appropriate expectations. Having such reasonable, informed expectations and

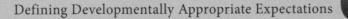

planning for children's developmental needs reduces the number of challenging behaviors teachers encounter in the classroom. When a challenging behavior occurs, an understanding of the child's developmental level, personality, strengths, and vulnerabilities empowers the teacher to plan interventions and approaches that will help the child function optimally.

Questions for Reflection

This chapter describes the importance of understanding reasonable, age-appropriate behaviors in young children. Consider the following questions as you think about your own experiences in working with young children.

1. If you work with infants and/or toddlers, did you gain any insights into the little ones with whom you work? How does Erikson's description of developmental phases support the interventions you already use?

2. How might your approach to the children change, based on your new knowledge or understanding of their development?

3. If you work with preschoolers, how do you respond to Erikson's description of that developmental stage? Does that description support the interventions you already use?

4. Is there a child who is similar in any way to one of the children described in the chapter? If so, did you discover any new ideas to consider regarding your work with the child?

5. How do the messages in this chapter regarding typical child development and age-appropriate expectations fit with what you already know and believe about what young children need?

6. Are there differences between what you already knew and what you read here? If so, how might this new information help you in the classroom?

7. If you feel it is appropriate, edit your list of goals and values that you created in Chapter One.

Creating the Classroom Environment

A major goal of preschool teachers is to encourage and support children's positive behaviors in their classrooms. While teachers prefer to have well-organized, attractively furnished, well-supplied classrooms, many may not see the connection between such classrooms and the behavior of the children in them. Although a teacher may have little control over some aspects of the classroom, such as the architecture of the space or funding for high-quality furniture, materials, and classroom repairs, she can shape the environment into one that is warm and welcoming for young children.

An attractive and functional physical environment is not only aesthetically pleasing but also supports young children's productive play and behavior. The environment functions as an adjunct teacher, pointing the way for children to find areas and materials to explore on their own or with peers. Well-organized and well-planned environments support children's ability to make good choices by giving them cues as to what kinds of activities are available and appropriate in which parts of the classroom.

Choosing Learning Spaces

Consider what defined activity areas you want in your preschool classroom. Think about the different areas of development that a classroom should address through experiential and play activities, and create spaces to support this learning. The following are some typical learning spaces:

● **Art Area:** Open-ended art explorations support children's oral language skills, fine motor development, self-confidence, and creative thinking. Provide a variety of art materials for children to explore, both independently and with teacher assistance.

Art explorations can be messy, so provide smocks and try to set up the area on a tiled floor rather than on carpet. If you have a sink, great! If not, provide a tub of water for easy hand washing. Offer lots of table space and, if possible, easels. Store art materials in easy-to-access containers organized to make cleanup simple.

- **Literacy Area:** As children's literacy skills emerge, they benefit from exposure to writing implements such as markers, crayons, pencils, fingers, chalk, and sticks; writing surfaces such as paper, envelopes, sand, chalkboards, and dry-erase boards; environmental print; and all sorts of age-appropriate books. Make the area inviting with low tables, shelves, easily accessed materials, and comfortable seating. Consider the placement of the area carefully, and set it up in a quiet space.

- **Science Area:** This area can change to reflect the explorations and interests of the children. Offer objects from the natural world that the children are learning about, and provide rulers, tape measures, magnifying glasses, scales, paper, pencils, and relevant books for the children to use.

- **Sensory Area:** Consider providing materials for sensory exploration, such as sand, playdough, and water, along with tubes, funnels, cookie cutters, and plastic implements. Sensory activities not only offer opportunities for science exploration but also soothe and calm young children. Often, children with mild sensory deficits will engage in challenging behaviors because they are seeking sensory stimulation. Providing sensory activities to meet these needs is likely to reduce inappropriate behavior.

- **Block Area:** Block play supports social-emotional and spatial learning, fine motor skills, creative thinking, and language development. Set this area up in a spot where the noise will not bother others and where the children will have space to create. Provide lots of blocks in a variety of sizes and materials, along with vehicles and toy people and animals.

- **Math Area:** Offer smaller manipulatives, such as Duplos, bristle blocks, LEGOs, tangrams, puzzles, and plastic numbers, all in organized containers on open shelves. Provide table space where the children can spread out the materials.

- **Dramatic Play Area:** This area can change as often as the children's imaginations. Provide costumes, toy housewares and tools, a table or tables and chairs, dolls, and other props. To keep interest high, consider rotating the themes, creating a home, a firehouse, a police station, a grocery store, a doctor's office, or any other idea the children may be interested in.

- **Music Area:** Offer a selection of musical instruments for the children to play. Provide CD players and a variety of music from around the world, and let the children explore music and movement. If possible, hang a large, unbreakable mirror in the area so children can see themselves move. Obviously, this area will be noisy, so place it far away from areas of quieter exploration.

- **Quiet Area:** Offer a space where children can go when they need to calm themselves or when they just need some time alone. Provide comfortable seating, books, quiet music, and soft lighting. Define the space with shelving, a rug, and perhaps an open tent or canopy.

- **Community Space:** Provide a large space for gathering at circle time or large group time. This area can do double duty as the gross motor area, as needed. Define the area with a large rug.

- **Gross Motor Area:** If you have the space, provide an area for an obstacle course, using mats, indoor climbers, fabric tunnels, or large cardboard boxes.

Arranging the Classroom

When you have chosen the areas you wish to feature in your classroom, reflect on the arrangement carefully. Set the children up for success by placing areas for quiet exploration near each other and far from the noisier areas. Place areas where messes are likely to happen in a part of the classroom where cleanup will be easy.

A few years ago, I consulted for a preschool where I observed a large classroom for four- and five-year-olds. I had been called in to observe a child who had difficulty following group expectations and who frequently got into trouble for misbehavior of various sorts. Before I could address this boy's behavior, however, the teacher and I needed to figure out how to arrange the classroom in a way that would maximize productive play.

I noticed that there was a particularly large, open space in the middle of the classroom with no apparent purpose. Children frequently ran around in this area, getting overstimulated and needing to be corralled by the teacher. The space itself gave a confusing message to children: It was not really large enough for gross motor play, yet it was clear of furniture and toys. The space communicated, "Come over here and run around!" The other areas of the classroom were poorly defined, making it difficult for the children to see their play options readily.

When classrooms are organized and laid out in ways that make sense, young children are more likely to engage in productive play and to display fewer behavior problems. For example, place the block area in a defined space where the children can build without worrying that their creations will be knocked over accidentally. Choose a spot away from the classroom door and from high-traffic areas. Place it in an area where noisy construction play will not bother children who are looking at books or engaging in some needed quiet time.

One area that can be extremely useful in preschool classrooms is a place for a child to go when she needs to calm down. Such an area should be comfortable and soothing. Include soft seating such as a beanbag chair, a few soft stuffed animals for cuddling, large pillows, and perhaps some soft music and lighting. Frequently, teachers use their reading areas as calming spaces, and that can work if the reading area is not already occupied by other children. If you wish, include age-appropriate books on feelings; note, however, that if the upset child is likely to throw something, you would want to limit her access to hard objects.

Ideally, this space should not be completely open to another play area. Consider defining the space with a shelving unit or cabinet and a rug. For safety, a child in the calming area should be visible to the teacher at all times but separated from the hubbub of the classroom. Having a calming space where a child can retreat when upset sends a comforting message to the children. It communicates understanding, nurturing, acceptance, and patience.

Selecting and Organizing Materials

The types of toys and materials that teachers use in the classroom are critical components of high-quality play. Materials that lend themselves to open-ended play and exploration are preferable to those that have only one use. Provide, for example, a wide variety of art materials that the children can explore in any way they wish.

The Reggio Emilia movement, modeled after the approach to preschool education developed in the villages surrounding the city of the same name in Italy, has inspired preschools worldwide with its approach to child-centered, open-ended explorations. There are a number of components to this approach, but one aspect is the way children are encouraged to connect with a topic of interest through painting, drawing, sculpture, writing, and dramatic play. Not only are their classrooms beautifully designed and arranged, but also the wide variety of materials for children to explore both on their own and with the teacher's guidance is quite impressive.

Classrooms with large amounts of toys and materials piled in plastic bins and on open shelves around the classrooms tend to feel overstimulating and messy. Carefully select the materials that you want the children to use. Store materials you plan to bring out at a later time in closed cabinets or bins out of the children's sight and reach.

Display the available materials attractively in clearly labeled containers. Well-organized, open shelving helps children learn where to find the items they want and where to store them when they are finished. Support young children's emerging literacy skills by creating labels that incorporate both the words and a photo of the items that belong in a container. The children will then be able to put things away in their proper spots.

A well-organized, well-supplied, attractive classroom communicates a welcoming message to children. It invites them to make independent decisions about what they would like to explore and offers engaging materials to help them dig deeply into subjects that interest them.

Children often become bored with the same old things week after week. Rotate the materials, removing and storing items that the children no longer use and replenishing supplies of frequently used materials. For example, in the sensory area, change the materials regularly to keep interest high. Hide dinosaurs or other toys in the sand; vary the sensory material using ice, shaving cream, sawdust, clean mud, feely goop, or colored water; and provide a variety of tools such as funnels, plastic tubing, shovels, scoops, and rakes. In any one center, discard or repair any broken items, and provide enough materials so that a number of children can play in the same area and have adequate supplies.

If you notice that an area is particularly popular, consider what the children are learning there and provide other materials that meet the same need. For example, in one classroom I visited, I noticed that large numbers of children wanted to play at the water table. Four children at a time could be accommodated there, and the teacher repeatedly told other children who approached that they needed to find something else to do until there was an opening at the water table. Having to ask large numbers of children to wait is a signal that something is not working well. There were no other sensory activities available in the classroom that day, so the children who wanted to play with water were forced to find nonsensory activities to do. In this case, a simple solution would be to offer other sensory materials for the children to explore. The teacher could provide playdough, fingerpaints, water in a bin, or sand on a tray. Waiting a few minutes for a spot to open up at a play area is acceptable, but if several children are crowding in an area, the teacher should pay attention; reflect on the center, the children, and the environment; and make some adjustments.

During a consultation at another preschool, a teacher expressed her concern that the children were not using the dramatic play area. The area was arranged to promote housekeeping play. When I took a look, I noticed that several naked dolls were piled up on the doll bed, and there were no blankets or pillows. The doll clothes were mixed in with the dress-up clothes, and all were thrown helter-skelter into a cabinet. The toy pots and pans and the pretend food were mixed up together in the refrigerator and sink. It was a mess!

I suggested that the teachers organize the area, put the materials neatly into child-accessible bins, and label each bin with words and photos. Children love to undress dolls, yet dressing them is a little more difficult. We agreed that the teachers would dress the dolls at the end of each day. The teachers provided a blanket and pillow for the doll bed and found some extra dolls, in case a handful of children wanted to play with them on a particular day, storing them in a cabinet until they were needed. They cleaned up the area during nap time, and the children resumed their dramatic play that very afternoon. The neat and organized space drew the children to the area.

One might wonder whether it matters all that much that children are not using the dramatic play area. After all, children need the opportunity to make choices regarding their play, and not playing in the dramatic play area is a choice. Keep in mind, though, that the dramatic play area is often the hub of elaborate fantasy play, which supports social and emotional learning in young children. If the area is unused, the children are missing out on important play experiences.

Keep the dramatic play area fresh and appealing by varying the themes. Consider creating an ice cream parlor, a veterinarian's office, or a pizza restaurant. Create prop boxes for different themes, and transform the area into something new and different when you notice the children's interest beginning to wane. It is not hard to get materials from local restaurants, such as old menus, to use for play. Old blue work shirts can become police uniforms, laminated cardboard stars can be badges, pads of paper with pencils can be used for taking orders in restaurants or for writing tickets at the police department.

When you pull out a prop box, set up the area for the children. Although the idea of supporting children's independent choices is a good one, it helps them to see a hint of what is possible with the new props. For example, if the pizza restaurant prop box is out, put a checkered tablecloth on the table and set out some menus. Leave the rest of the materials in the prop box for the children to sort through and decide how they want to use them. Such visual cues stimulate the children's imagination and draw them in.

Engaging children in high-quality, compelling play activities is a top priority. Keep your eyes open for any necessary changes to ensure that children's needs are being met through explorations that work for them.

Teaching Children to Use and Care for Their Classroom

Brain research tells us that preschoolers' brains are rapidly developing new neural pathways and making connections that help them understand and master their experiences and feelings. A supportive environment with the right balance of stimulation and comfort enables these connections to flourish.

The Montessori approach, developed by Maria Montessori in the early twentieth century, emphasizes the importance of using the physical environment to support young children's learning. A significant amount of attention is paid to the organization and setup of the materials and the environment. The children also are taught how to care for, respect, properly use, and store play materials.

Many children come to preschool not knowing how to use and care for play materials. They need their teachers to demonstrate and explain what to do. When children understand what materials are available, how to use them, and how the items are stored, they will be much more likely to care for them.

Some children, for example, might need direct teacher supervision at the water table so that they can learn to use the table without becoming too overstimulated. For some children, having an individual bin with water or sand and some play materials might be a better choice to help maintain a sense of calm in the activity. Observe the children as they interact with materials, reflect on what you see happening, and consider the possible underlying reasons for any challenging behaviors or misuse of the materials. This will lead you to consider ways to provide solutions that can help a child behave more positively. Help children make good choices for play. Provide visual cues for what could be done in a particular area. For example, in the manipulatives area, set the bin of Duplos on the table and stick a few blocks together to give the children an idea of what could happen there.

Use the gross motor area or community area to incorporate various forms of gross motor play indoors throughout the day. Young children need to move. They will be better able to focus if they have at least sixty minutes of physical activity each day, as recommended by the Centers for Disease Control and Prevention. Also, many preschool-age children, boys especially, learn through movement, or kinesthetically. Children need outlets for their energy, both indoors and out.

Many teachers feel comfortable with fine motor activities, indoor voices, and quieter styles of play, preferences that may play a role in the expectations of what indoor play in preschool classrooms should look like. While the large block area provides some opportunities for gross motor experiences, there are other ways to bring gross motor play indoors. Often teachers find themselves reminding boys to quiet their bodies, use walking feet, and refrain from wrestling with their friends in the classroom. This tells us that we need to find more ways to meet children's needs for gross motor experiences indoors on a regular basis.

Juan is a four-year-old who loves to play in a boisterous, physically adventurous way in the classroom. Sometimes he gets himself into dangerous situations, such as climbing on the block cabinet and jumping off. He knows what the rules are but struggles to contain his need for physical movement and gross motor play. His teacher is quite exasperated with Juan and wants to figure out how to contain him and keep him safe in the classroom.

All children need opportunities to engage in gross motor activities, both indoors and outdoors. Juan may need more gross motor activity than the rest of the children. There are a variety of options for offering him safer opportunities to move his body at school. One would be to create obstacle courses in the gross motor area using tumbling mats. Juan could jump, roll, or hop across in a variety of ways. Add a fabric tunnel or large, open appliance boxes for Juan and all of the children to crawl through. By providing clear directions about how the obstacle course is to be used and by supervising him, the teacher can communicate her understanding for Juan's need for physical activity.

Another easy gross motor game uses two masking-tape lines placed a couple of feet apart on the floor. The children can run, jump, or hop between the lines a certain number of times. Set the taped lines farther apart, and add a beanbag toss to the game. The children can run back and forth, tossing beanbags into a plastic bin. No matter which gross motor activities you choose to incorporate into your classroom, remember to keep the activities structured and well supervised. Clearly communicate your expectations to the children to set them up for success.

Successful Scheduling and Transitions

When you have reflected on the learning spaces you want to feature in your classroom and have arranged the areas carefully, supplying organized, accessible, and developmentally appropriate materials, you are ready to encourage the children's explorations. One of the most important decisions the teacher makes in regard to the operation of her classroom is how she schedules the day. Like the physical architecture and organization of the classroom itself, the schedule provides the framework for how the children move through each day. Help the children understand what the schedule will be. Provide visual cues such as a picture schedule, and refer to it often.

Think carefully about when activities will take place, and consider what is developmentally appropriate for the children you teach. For example, young children cannot sit still and focus on a story for more than a few minutes at a time. Do not plan to read a story that will take 15 to 20 minutes to finish in one sitting during circle time. Instead, break the story into short segments and read it over several circle times. If the children tend to struggle with focusing during a fine motor activity, consider a short dance break beforehand to help them get their wiggles out.

Transitions are challenging for young children. Many children may feel at loose ends, insecure, and anxious between finishing one activity and starting another, and they may exhibit challenging behaviors. Limit the number of transitions in your schedule, having as few as possible. Give the children a warning a few minutes before the end of an activity, so that they can get used to the idea that soon they will need to stop playing and move on to something new.

Each transition presents its own challenges. Cleaning up after free play, for example, can be difficult. It is hard to stop playing when one is having a good time, and playing with materials is more fun than putting them away. Encourage peer modeling and recognize children's efforts to help. Consider singing a song to acknowledge children who are helping: "Joey is cleaning! LaKeisha is cleaning! Sara is cleaning!" Although such acknowledgement can be motivating, guard against stigmatizing children who may struggle with this transition. Avoid creating a competitive environment in which children want to outdo one another. Experiment with reinforcers to see what works well with your group. Support the children as they learn to handle transitions. For example, some children might do better if they help you to clean up a particular area of the room. Others can work independently or with a friend.

Arrivals and departures often are particularly stressful transitions for young children. Consider ways to make these times a little easier. For example, one preschool organized the morning so that the three-year-olds started their day with outdoor time. Families brought their children to the teachers on the playground, then said their goodbyes. This eliminated the need for the teachers to get the children bundled up to go outdoors later in the morning, and it also helped the children handle their feelings about separation. The same preschool scheduled pickup time for the four-year-olds outside, as well. Families picked up their children at the playground, which eliminated the need to cajole the children to get their coats on and leave the classroom.

Another challenge during transitions is the issue of wait time. Young children struggle when they have to wait for more than a few minutes with nothing to do. Consider your schedule carefully, and strive to limit wait times wherever possible. If children must wait, provide something to hold their attention and act as an outlet for their energy. For example, if the group is headed outside after clean-up time, some children may be ready to go out the door and may find themselves waiting for the children who are still helping. Consider offering a transitional activity such as a selection of books or a basket of fidgets kept near the door, or sing a song or do a fingerplay together.

This approach can work well at large group time, too. If, for example, the children must wash their hands before they join the group for circle time, some children likely will dawdle at the sink, and others may need extra help with handwashing. To keep the early arrivers from getting squirmy and disruptive, provide them with small vehicles to play with on the rug while they wait. When all the children have joined the group, consider beginning with a music and movement activity to help the children get their wiggles out. At the end of circle time, use a transitional activity to help the children move on to the next part of the day. Call the children who are wearing green, for example, to move to centers first; or, ask all the children who have blue shoes to move to centers first. In this way, the children will transition calmly.

Working with young children requires that caregivers not only follow carefully thought-out schedules, but also that they remain flexible and willing to make adjustments as needed. When the classroom environment is structured to support children's developing sense of initiative and to help them gain confidence in their ability to carry out ideas and impact their world, the children learn to function successfully. Use the environment as an adjunct teacher to plan ahead for success. Reflect on ways that you can create a nurturing classroom that supports children's explorations and learning.

Questions for Reflection

1. Consider your classroom structure.

    - Do you think your room arrangement supports high-quality, productive play?
    - Are the learning areas of the classroom well defined and laid out so that the children readily know what kinds of activities are available to them?
    - Can the children move easily among the learning spaces?
    - Are the spaces for quiet exploration placed far from spaces where noisier play takes place?
    - Do the children clearly understand what areas are available to them and what areas are off limits?
    - If the children have difficulty moving through the classroom and making good choices for play, how can you rearrange the classroom to alleviate the problem?

2. Consider the materials available to the children.

    - Are the materials and toys in good repair?
    - Are the materials well organized and neatly displayed?
    - Are the containers clearly labeled, so the children know where materials belong?
    - Do you edit the number of materials available, so the children are not overwhelmed with too many choices?
    - Do you rotate the materials frequently to spark the children's interest?
    - Do you provide options for sensory exploration, such as a sand-and-water table, playdough, fingerpaint, or fidgets?

3. Consider your daily classroom schedule.

    - Can the children clearly understand the schedule and anticipate each activity?
    - Are the order and length of activities developmentally appropriate?
    - Do you limit the number of transitions?
    - Do the children move through the transitions comfortably, or are some transitions more challenging than others?
    - What kind of changes or adjustments might you make to help the children transition more smoothly?

4. If you feel it is appropriate, edit your list of goals and values that you created in Chapter One.

Connecting with Families

Most early childhood educators understand the importance of connecting with families and forming partnerships to meet children's learning needs. Yet, envisioning what such relationships should look like and how to achieve them is not always entirely clear. The essence of positive family member–teacher partnerships can be summed up in three words: *communication*, *respect*, and *trust*.

When family members feel respected and receive clear, ongoing communication from a teacher who is genuinely interested in their perceptions and opinions, there is a much higher likelihood of parental trust, cooperation, and involvement. Connecting with family members begins when they arrive to enroll their children in your program. Administrators can discuss not only the program's philosophy and approach but also the parents' concerns, priorities, and goals for their children.

Begin with the Intake Process

Administrators should use the intake process to fully inform family members about the program's rules, practices, and school expectations. Both teachers and administrators need to take the time to learn not only about a child's developmental history but also about the family's cultural background, family traditions, home language, and educational expectations. Some programs use intake forms to ask about recipes, stories, and songs the family might feel comfortable sharing with the children. This sends a message at the beginning of a child's experience in the program that parental involvement is valued and welcomed. Many

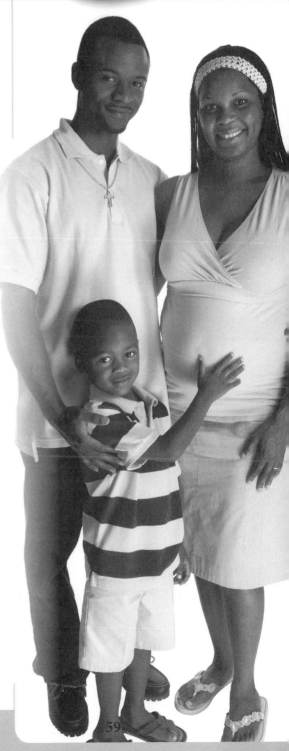

59

programs include a question such as "What do you hope our program will do for your child?" on their intake forms. This opens the door for families to express their wishes for their children's academic-skill acquisition and provides an opportunity for an open dialogue on the program's approach, values, and practices; developmentally appropriate approaches to teaching math and literacy skills; and the value of high-quality play experiences. Key to establishing communication with a family is the face-to-face meeting. Having this happen during the intake process or very shortly thereafter gives the administrator and teacher the opportunity to send a message of validation and communicates the program's interest in a mutually respectful partnership. (For a sample intake form, see the Appendix on page 135.)

Jorge is a three-year-old who has just entered a full-day preschool program. He is hesitant to engage in play activities, preferring to observe the action. His teacher, Michael, notices Jorge watching the children sliding at outdoor time, and he approaches Jorge. "Your mom told me that your favorite park is the one down the block from your house. Does that park have a slide?"

Jorge's eyes light up. "Yes! It's bigger than this one!"

Michael encourages Jorge to try the one at school and tell him what he thinks about it.

As Jorge climbs the ladder, he says, "My slide has more steps!" He slides down happily.

Jorge's teacher is able to use the information he gained from the intake form Jorge's parents filled out. Learning about Jorge's life at home enables Michael to help Jorge bridge his feeling of comfort and safety at home with his new life at school. This kind of empathic bridging helps to build trust. When Jorge's mom picks him up at the end of the day, Michael can share the information about their conversation about the park and let her know that Jorge got directly involved in the outdoor play at school. It is likely that Jorge's family will be relieved and grateful he feels comfortable at his new school, and the trust will begin to grow.

What other avenues are available to teachers to lay the foundation for positive working relationships with families? Clear communication regarding classroom values, practices, and routines is essential, and it is especially helpful if teachers communicate these messages in a variety of ways. Create a short list of classroom practices and routines that require cooperation from families, and explain the list clearly when a child enters the program. Consider including information on policies such as the following:

- Keeping a change of clothes at school
- Handling toys that a child brings from home
- Bringing in snacks and other food
- Toileting policies
- Nap-time practices
- Classroom pets
- Birthdays and other celebrations

Rather than simply handing the list to the family, discuss it with them if possible and give them an opportunity to ask questions. Enrolling one's child in a preschool program is detailed and can be a little overwhelming. Communicate your classroom expectations verbally and in writing, and, later, reiterate them in newsletters or emails. However, even the most organized approach to communicating with families, delivered in the most friendly and respectful way, will not always meet with compliance. Here is where the teacher's ingenuity comes in quite handy.

Madeline is an energetic three-year-old who loves experimenting with paints. Despite wearing the required smock, she frequently manages to get paint on her clothes and needs a change. Her family has not supplied extra clothes for Madeline in a while, and the teacher often must search for dry socks or a shirt for Madeline to put on after painting.

Her teacher approaches Madeline's mom at the end of the school day and enthusiastically reports, "Madeline is a budding Picasso! She absolutely loves to experiment with and explore paint! She makes at least three gorgeous, colorful paintings a day, and I am so impressed with her use of color! As you know, she also tends to get paint on her clothes. Can we work together to create a plan for replenishing her supply of extra clothes each day? We need to make sure she's dry and comfortable when painting time is over."

In this case, the teacher's positive regard for Madeline goes a long way in engaging the parent's cooperation. For some parents, however, having enough extra clothes to leave at school might be a challenge. Use your judgment and sensitivity, and utilize the school's emergency extra-clothes stash if you think it is warranted. Your knowledge of and ability to reflect on each child's individual circumstances will guide you in these interactions.

Keep the Communication Flowing

Another critical aspect of communication is letting families know how their child's day went. Sometimes this is made more difficult because the teacher who is with the child most of the day is not the teacher in charge at pickup time. Some programs have the child's primary teacher write a short note about the child's day, which gets handed to the parent at pickup time. If the parent or guardian is not the person who picks up the child or if the child uses alternate transportation, then work with the family to communicate regularly and maintain a positive connection. For some families, a weekly phone call or email communication can support that connection.

Be specific in your feedback for the family: "Troy helped Maria put away the crayons when they spilled on the floor. And, he had a great time playing basketball during outdoor time." Families need to know what their children are doing at school. Let them know positive details, so that when a more negative report is necessary, they will be more receptive. You will have established a trusting relationship, and they will be less likely to react defensively. If you are struggling with a child who is exhibiting challenging behavior, communicate a couple of positive details about the child each day.

This kind of specific, detailed communication is gratifying and informative for the parent to hear, and it also sets a model for the kind of information the teacher would like to receive from the parent. Teachers like to be informed by families when something important has happened at home. Anything that might affect the child's day at school and will allow the teacher to better understand the child is valuable information. Such information is more likely to be shared when the family receives regular, detailed feedback from the teacher.

Encourage Family Participation

Invite family members to participate in the program by sharing favorite family stories or cultural traditions. This is a great way to demonstrate respect and to build trust between home and school. Some parents are more available to spend time at school than others, but even those whose time may be quite limited may be able to share a favorite holiday book or a recipe for a traditional meal or treat. Make an effort to send the message to the families that their life experiences are valued at school and the teachers would enjoy the opportunity to share them with the children.

One program I have worked with included a Swedish family who celebrates May Day each year with special games. They decorate a maypole with long ribbons and dance around it. The family asked if it would be all right to share their celebration with the children. The teachers agreed and planned a May Day celebration, complete with a special dessert.

Another program invited a child whose family had returned home to Jamaica over the winter break to share her experiences with the class. She described swimming in the ocean and brought in some of the seashells she had gathered on the beach. Since this program was located in the Chicago area, the children were intrigued at the idea of swimming in the ocean in winter. The teacher picked up on their interest and decided to create Jamaica in the classroom. He decorated the classroom, hanging fishnets on the walls and putting plastic sea creatures in them. He hid seashells in the sand table and played Jamaican music, shared by the child's mother, in the background while the children went about their usual routine. The child's mother prepared plantains for the children to taste, and the teacher even filled a small baby pool for the children to play in!

Not only did the teacher build a creative emergent curriculum in which the children were deeply engaged, but he also cemented the bonds between this child, her mother, and the larger school community. What a lovely way to honor the diversity of cultures and experiences!

Such special parental-participation events are successful only when carefully planned by the teacher. Work with the family members to organize the event so that the children can participate successfully. It is worth the effort. Sharing different cultures and experiences helps to build a sense of community and teaches children about differences and acceptance.

Build the Trust

In addition to direct parental participation in activities at school, there are many other ways teachers can demonstrate the kind of respect and caring that builds trust. Teachers are usually quite comfortable with greeting each child as she enters the classroom in the morning, but do not forget to greet the families as well. Making a point of greeting each family member individually sends the message that families are valued. Even a quick "Good morning, Helen!" will do. Such quick connections let the families know that your concern does not begin and end with the children.

Separation

Another opportunity for building trust is through your handling of separation feelings, both the child's and the family member's. Early childhood educators can do a tremendous service to families by helping them understand the importance of the process of separation. Supporting children and families to successfully move through this process helps cement family bonds and creates new ones with the school program. Teachers and parents often try to hurry through the separation process; however, such an approach bypasses a significant opportunity to support healthy psychological development.

For many children, entering a preschool program represents their first experience with spending an extended period of time away from their families. They will be discovering a new world outside their home environment, with new adults as well as new physical spaces. While this can be exciting and fun, children often have anxiety about the change from the familiar. Allow children to experience and express their feelings and to receive comfort from supportive adults so that they can master their feelings more fully. Do not attempt to bypass their feelings by rushing the separation process.

To better understand a child's feelings about separation, it can be helpful to compare a child's experience to an adult's separation feelings in her own life. When a friend visits from out of town, the time spent together is valued deeply. It is not unusual on the night before the friend's departure for the adult to feel some trepidation, anxiety, or sadness. These feelings are an adult version of the separation feelings a child feels. For most adults, once the friend has departed, the sadness or anxiety gradually dissipates as the adult resumes her regular routine; the anticipation of the separation is the most painful part. It is very much the same for children: The anticipation and the moment of separation are the hardest to bear. This is why so many teachers try to rush that moment of separation. Their intentions are honorable, but for children to master these feelings, they must experience and work through them. When children are allowed to experience and express their feelings and receive comfort from supportive adults, they master them more fully than when teachers attempt to bypass them by rushing the process.

There are a variety of strategies that help children and families master such feelings:

- **Plan for a gradual entry into preschool.** Encourage a family member to stay with the child at the beginning of school for a period of time before leaving. Programs can accomplish this in a variety of ways. Some have the children attend the first day of preschool with half of their classmates and the parents, for a shortened first day. Other programs invite the parents to stay with their children for half of the first day, and then provide chairs in the back of the classroom for parents of children who might need them to be present for more than one day. Although many children adjust to preschool readily, others need more time. Be sensitive to each child's needs. If a parent is unable to stay with a child, encourage her to ask a grandparent or other close family member to come in to ease the child's transition. If another family member is not available, suggest that the child be picked up a little early for the first week or so. Think creatively to find solutions that work for each situation.
- **Support the parents, too.** Sometimes, the child seems to be making an excellent adaptation to the program, yet the family member wants to hang around and remain available to the child "just in case." In such situations, it may be the parent who needs the support in separating. It is very helpful in such situations to ask that a director

or staff member be available to help the family member with the transition. Reassure the hovering parent that the child is making a nice adjustment to preschool and is ready for him to leave the classroom. Give the parent time to say a quick goodbye before he goes.

- **Establish a morning goodbye routine.** Even for the child who does not seem to need much help with this, it is good for children to say goodbye to their families in the morning rather than having them just slip out the door. Slipping out the door can seem like an easier solution when the child is already engaged in play; however, some children will become quite upset a little while later when they look around and see that their parents have disappeared. Establish consistent goodbye routines that the children can depend on. For the child who insists on three more kisses or one more puzzle, for example, it can help to know that the plan is one puzzle, two kisses, and a goodbye. Communicate with the families about establishing a simple goodbye routine, and support them in following the routine consistently.

- **Encourage the families to send in a family photo.** Many programs ask parents to bring in a picture of their family to keep at school. These pictures can be made into a collage that is posted on a wall of the classroom, or the children can keep their photos in their cubbies to look at whenever they need a little extra reassurance. Alternatively, consider taking a photo of each child with a family member or members at the beginning of the program. Then, print it out to keep at school.

- **Provide children's books about attachment and separation.** Reading books about separation validates children's feelings and gives the message that such feelings are understood, accepted, and can be mastered. There are many books that address separation; examples include *The Kissing Hand* by Audrey Penn and *The Invisible String* by Patrice Karst.

- **Talk about family members with the children.** Often, teachers are reluctant to speak of family members at school, especially as the children are initially adjusting to the program, for fear of upsetting the children. However, when teachers do not mention families at school, children can get the message that they are not supposed to be thinking about their families. It is reassuring to say something such as, "Mommy is at the office now. Do you think she might be working on a computer?" Or, at lunchtime, mention, "I wonder what Daddy is having for lunch today at his work." Reinforce for children the idea that their thoughts about their loved ones are acceptable and that their attachment to their families is valued.

- **Encourage families to write notes to their children.** For children who have intense feelings about separation, additional strategies may be necessary. Ask a family member to write a goodbye note to the child that can be kept at school and read to the child as needed. The note could reassure him:

Mommy will be working at the store today while you are at school, helping people buy food for their families. I know you will have fun doing art projects, hearing stories, and playing outside. I will be so happy to see you after snack time this afternoon. I will give you a great big hug! I love you lots and lots!

If the child is feeling lonely, read the note to him.

- **Let the children dictate notes to their family members.** If a child is sad or angry or wants his mommy or daddy right away, the teacher can offer to write a note to the parent for the child. Whatever the child wants to say is acceptable; write the note just as the child dictates it, without judging:

TEACHER: What do you want to say to Mommy? I will write down your words, and we can put the note in your locker so that she can read it as soon as it's time for pickup.

CHILD: I want you with me all the time at school! I want to stay at home with you and the baby and not come to school!

By writing the child's words verbatim without comment, you will validate the child's feelings, even though acting on those feelings in the way the child wants is not always possible. Read the note back to the child, reassuring him that you understand how hard it is to be at school when Mommy is not there. Then, help him find something fun to do with you, such as a sensory activity, which can be soothing for children who are feeling upset.

All of these strategies are geared to supporting children and parents in mastering feelings about separation. When this process is handled with sensitivity, children make better adjustments to the school setting and families develop trust in the teachers. Note that it is not at all unusual for children who adapt easily to a program in the beginning to suddenly begin crying at separation after an illness, a school break, or even a long weekend at home with the family. Such episodes are all part of the process of healthy psychological development, and your patience and understanding will go a long way toward helping the child move forward more quickly.

Challenging Family Members

Teachers can sometimes feel frustrated with aspects of their relationships with parents. In dealing with a challenging family member, strive to understand the person's perspective and to keep the lines of communication open.

There are many possible reasons why a parent might not initially feel comfortable and trusting of teachers and schools. For example, some families may have very clear ideas about how children should be brought up. Some parents may have had difficult experiences in their own education. Some may come from cultural backgrounds that are very different from that of the teacher, with beliefs, expectations, and childrearing practices that the teacher must strive to understand. Establishing and maintaining open lines of communication, beginning at the intake process, will help parents and teachers find ways to work together and resolve any differences. Remember that you share a common goal—that the child be successful.

Much of a parent's reluctance or resistance likely will have nothing to do with the teacher. Generally, the parent's feelings stem from her own life experiences. Move forward in a positive manner and seek to find common ground. When teachers and directors work toward building positive connections with parents whose communication or stance may initially be somewhat challenging, it goes a long way toward overcoming any negativity.

Karen is a three-year-old who does not nap at home. She attends a full-day program that schedules a regular rest period each day, per the state's licensing requirements. Her parents do not want Karen to take a nap at school, fearing that she will not be able to get to sleep at night if she naps during the afternoon.

Even children who do not usually nap at home sometimes will fall asleep at school during nap time, when the lights are low and they are expected to stay on their cots without play materials to entertain them. This may lead to some children's bedtime becoming more complicated, and parents who are exhausted at the end of a long workday are not pleased when their little ones are unable to fall asleep at a reasonable hour.

One program found a creative solution to take into account both family and program needs. The children who no longer took naps at home were sent to their cots last, after the others had mostly settled down. Their parents prepared special backpacks with some materials the children could use quietly at rest time, such as sticker books, special markers, dot-to-dot books, and so on. These backpacks were only for rest time, so that the children would view them as special. In addition, these children were the first invited to get up at the end of rest time. In this way, rest time was shortened a bit for these children, they participated in quiet activities, and they were less likely to actually sleep.

Henry is running a fever and seems pretty miserable. The preschool calls his mother, who comes to pick him up a couple of hours later, looking harried. The director reminds her that a child who has a fever cannot return to school until the fever has been gone for at least twenty-four hours.

The next morning, the mom brings Henry back to school and hurriedly heads for the door when the teacher attempts to explain that the child cannot return so soon. The mother insists that his fever went away the previous evening and he is feeling much better. She then explains that she absolutely has to show up for work that day or she might lose her job.

Teachers do empathize with parents who may not have good backup plans for child care when the child is sick. However, when children come to school sick, other children are likely to be infected. In this case, the teacher gently but firmly insisted that the parent take the child home. Later at a parent meeting, the director reviewed the school's policy on keeping sick children at home to prevent illness from spreading to the other children.

It is easier to maintain positive relationships with families when limits such as these are consistently enforced and there is a solid base of trust and mutual respect between home and school. Partnerships with families may require a willingness to be flexible and to adapt at times to specific circumstances; tweaks to school practices can be accomplished without harming the program. When such adjustments are not possible, it is the teacher's responsibility to be clear about that and to explain why adjustments cannot be made.

Will is a fussy eater. When he does not like the lunch menu for the day, his parents send in a peanut butter sandwich, in spite of the school policy banning all peanut products because of allergy concerns.

Many programs have banned peanut butter because of the common problem of peanut allergies. In this case, an exception to the rule cannot be made, since it could put other children at risk. The teacher needs to explain the reason for the rule and to assure the parent that there are food options available that are likely to appeal to the child.

Taylor has asthma, and his attacks are often triggered by cold weather. His parents have asked that he be kept inside to play on cold days.

This is a tough situation. Although some children are more vulnerable to asthma attacks in cold weather, most programs do not have the staffing to provide an adult to stay with a child indoors when the rest of the class is playing outside. In this case, the teacher explained the problem to the parents and worked with them to come up with a solution. They discussed a number of options:

- letting the child choose quieter activities outdoors rather than running around,
- giving him an asthma treatment before outdoor time, or
- having him be the last child to go out and the first to come back in on cold days.

In most cases, the schedule of the day and the staffing patterns cannot be changed to accommodate one child. Yet, with careful discussion and planning, the program and parents were able to make some minor accommodations that worked for everyone.

Communicating a willingness to take parental concerns seriously and to make efforts to adapt the program to meet family needs reinforces respect and trust. Schools that convey the value of paying attention to parental concerns, ideas, and needs have a more satisfied, engaged, and cooperative family population. Valuing parental concerns does not always translate into doing exactly what a parent may want in every situation, but it does mean paying attention to parents' opinions and working with them to find solutions. High-quality preschools practice this commitment to partnership with parents every day.

Sometimes cultural expectations differ between a family and a program. Such situations need to be handled especially delicately so as not to offend a family, but at the same time maintain the principles and values associated with the school's program. For example, in some cultures, gender roles are quite strictly defined. It is important not to make assumptions and judgments about specific societies and cultures, however, because even within each culture there often are exceptions.

Four-year-old Miza loves to play with blocks of all kinds. Her teacher, Mrs. Pappas, admires her constructions and comments to her that perhaps she will become an architect when she grows up. Her parents come to talk with the teacher about this when Miza proudly repeats her compliments. They inform her that architecture is not an appropriate career for a girl, and they ask that Mrs. Pappas not encourage Miza's interest in playing with blocks.

One of the responsibilities of preschool educators is to respect families' ideas and requests whenever possible, but another equally important responsibility is to provide young children with the broadest possible array of opportunities for learning within the classroom. This situation was a conundrum for the teacher. How could she respect the parents' authority and values and continue to honor the precepts of contemporary early childhood education?

The teacher acknowledged her lack of understanding of gender-role expectations in their culture and apologized if anything she said to Miza was culturally offensive, as that was not intentional. She explained that the preschool program in which Miza is enrolled gives the children the freedom to explore the classroom, make choices about their play, and use play materials in productive ways. She commented about the learning-standard goals and benchmarks that are being addressed through Miza's play with blocks and how such play is preparing her for later success in school. She agreed not to talk with Miza about possible future career plans if that is offensive to the parents, but she explained that she cannot prevent Miza from making play choices that are meaningful and productive. The parents appreciated the teacher's humility and willingness to discuss the issue with them. They found her explanations about how play is preparing Miza to be successful in later school experiences to be very helpful, and they agreed to let Miza continue to use all of the classroom's play materials.

Had the teacher focused on Western ideas about what girls should be able to pursue professionally, she surely would have alienated these parents. By meeting them halfway and explaining the value of choosing developmentally appropriate play activities in preschool, she was able to keep the parents connected to the program and allow Miza to continue to enjoy her play at school.

Drop-off and pickup are important opportunities for teachers to communicate with family members and for families to connect with their children. Mr. Hayes is frustrated to find that many of his students' parents are using cell phones while they drop off or pick up their children. The center's policy clearly asks that family members put their cell phones away before entering.

Because interpersonal connections at the beginning and end of the day are important, it is essential that parental cell phone use be limited when entering the classroom. Programs accomplish this difficult task in many different ways, by posting reminder signs just outside the classroom door, by communicating nonverbally to parents who may be on the phone that it is time to put it down, or with verbal reminders. One program I visited posted a sign that read, "Put your cell phone away so that your child will have a good day!" Be firm with family members who may ignore the more gentle reminders. A teacher can redirect a chatting parent to take the child outside into the hall until he is finished with his conversation, saying, "Can't wait to greet Samantha today! As soon as you're finished with your call, please bring her into the classroom!"

Sharing Difficult Information

One of the more challenging aspects of working with families is the issue of how and when to share concerns regarding a child's development. This can include concerns about impulsiveness, patterns of inappropriate behavior, or potential developmental delays, each of which requires a carefully thought-out intervention plan. Families never like to hear that their child is not functioning optimally at school, so handle such conversations carefully.

If you have kept the communication flowing with families since they enrolled their children in the program, talking with a family about concerns for their child will be easier. If, for example, you have made a family aware of a pattern of inappropriate behavior, then talking with them about interventions for the child will not come as such a shock. However, if you have avoided sharing your concerns with the family, then trying to talk about intervention may be met with resistance. Mention concerns to parents early, rather than waiting until the concerns become more major and urgent.

Sam is a three-year-old who is only interested in lining up small toy cars on the large area rug or playing one specific computer game by himself. He becomes very upset if other children want to use the cars, and he refuses to have another child sit near him when he is playing the computer game.

He yells and flails his arms during transition times and seems uninterested in connecting with his teachers. Usually, children who are not ready to engage with their peers tend to prefer the adults in the classroom. Instead, Sam prefers to be alone, seemingly in his own world. He has very little language, and his play remains rigid and stereotyped.

After the first few weeks of the program, the teacher begins to be concerned that he might have a developmental disorder and may need an outside evaluation.

Because some children take longer to warm up to other children than others, if a child engages in this sort of play at the beginning of a school year, it does not necessarily raise red flags. However, if the behavior continues, then a conversation with the parents is warranted. Since teachers are not diagnosticians, the teacher must be very careful in how she communicates her concern to the parents. Reflect on what you know about the family and how strong your relationship is with them as you decide how to approach the subject.

One afternoon while the children are playing outside, Sam's mom arrives to pick him up. His teacher engages with her about Sam in a neutral way: "You know, I've noticed that Sam really loves the swings at outdoor time. Does he like going to the park?" His mom responds that he does. Then the teacher adds, "Sam is primarily interested in lining up the small cars in the classroom. Is this something he enjoys at home as well?" Sam's mom agrees that his favorite thing to do is to play with his cars. The teacher then replies, "Often when children are three years old, they enjoy a variety of play materials. Sam likes a particular computer game as well, but these two solitary activities are all he wants to do at school. I'd like to help him expand his repertoire of play interests, and we plan to work on introducing other materials in with the cars to see whether we can get Sam to engage with some other materials as well. We'll let you know how that goes. It's really a good thing for preschoolers to experiment with a variety of play activities."

The teacher has communicated her observations of Sam to his mother, providing her with information about how Sam is doing at preschool. She mentions that many three-year-olds enjoy a wider variety of play materials than Sam does, letting his mother know that she is noticing some differences between Sam's behavior and that of the other children. By avoiding the phrase *most three-year-olds* and choosing *many three-year-olds* instead, Sam's teacher is not saying that there is clearly something wrong with Sam. She explains the importance of preschoolers having a broad array of play experiences, and she tells Sam's mother what she plans to do to help Sam expand his interests.

Sam's teacher is not saying that there is clearly something wrong with Sam, but she is laying the groundwork for further communication along these lines. Letting the parent know that she has a specific intervention plan aimed at helping Sam expand his play interests is a critical component of her communication. It is reassuring for families to hear that the teacher has a strategy to help their child succeed. Depending on how disruptive Sam's reactions to transitions are, the teacher could have chosen to focus on that to discuss with the mom first. Such a discussion would have gone similarly, remaining low key and explaining what the teacher is doing to help Sam be calmer during transition times. If there are multiple areas of concern, focus on one area at a time in the beginning, so that parents do not feel barraged or overwhelmed with information that might frighten them. The goal is to inform parents in a timely fashion of issues that may need special attention. Help families feel that they are included and are respected. Doing so usually translates to family members being more likely to cooperate if further intervention or exploration is needed.

If a family member reacts to your concerns about a child by saying, "Oh, he never does that at home," consider that it is quite possible that he is being honest and that the child actually does not exhibit the behavior at home. A group setting with sixteen to twenty children is a very different environment from a home with one or two siblings. Even in cases in which the family member is not being totally honest, it is always helpful to assume positive intent on his part, recognizing that families usually want the best for their children. If they are unaware of or in denial about some aspect of their child's behavior, that stance serves some psychological purpose for them and is not specifically meant to cause trouble for the teacher. Continue to be respectful of the parent, and try to find other ways to enable the family to partner with you to address the behavior that is occurring at school.

Mrs. Parker tends to be brusque and somewhat physically rough with her child at pickup time. She is often in a hurry to get the child out of the classroom, saying, "Time to go, Brad!" and grabbing the child's arm to lead him out. This approach does not allow for time to check in with Mr. Conrad, Brad's teacher, nor does it allow Brad any time to transition from school to home, perhaps finishing a drawing or hearing the end of a story the teacher was reading. Frequently, Brad ends up crying as he is dragged out of the classroom at the end of the school day.

One of my favorite strategies for engaging parental cooperation is the "joining and leading" technique. Many teachers find this approach helpful in finding common ground with parents, especially in situations when part of the problem lies in the family member's attitude or behavior. The idea behind this strategy is that parents often are sensitive to feeling criticized. They may react defensively, wanting to explain themselves, disagree, or hold their ground when asked to change some aspect of their behavior in relation to their child. If the teacher's goal is to get the family member to do what the teacher believes is best, it is most effective if she presents her ideas in a way that makes that person or those persons feel respected and valued rather than criticized.

The "joining" part of the strategy means that one must find some aspect of what the family member is doing that one can join with and validate. Then, one can lead the person in a new direction. For this technique to work, the family member must feel that his style of nurturing has been accepted, valued, or validated in some way. Using this strategy requires teachers to find some aspect of the family member's behavior that is positive, for which the teacher can express her admiration and respect.

In the "leading" part, the teacher is able to engage the family member in considering making some change for the better in his behavior. The trick here is to make the teacher's message appear to be primarily the valuing and validating message, and for the change to appear to be simply an enhancement of what the family member already is doing and not really a fundamental change. He should experience the teacher's suggestion as an offer of a way for him to be even more successful in achieving his own goal.

Mr. Conrad sends Mrs. Parker an email to ask her to come by a little early one afternoon that week to talk briefly about the end-of-the-day routine at school. Mr. Conrad arranges to have another staff member cover his class for a short time so that he can speak with Mrs. Parker in a small conference room.

He greets her in a friendly manner and asks how her day has gone. Mrs. Parker replies, "It was really busy, but I'm here." He thanks her for taking the time to meet with him and assures her that he will not take long.

"I've been thinking a lot about the end-of-the-day routine with Brad, and I realize that you want Brad to respect your authority. When you tell him that it's time to go, you want him to listen with no nonsense. I respect that aspect of parenting. It's very important for children to understand that their parents are authority figures and that they need to cooperate with them. You are very clear with Brad, and it is helpful for children to see their parents being consistent. I've also noticed that frequently Brad gets upset and starts to cry when it is time to leave, which is hard for everyone. I think it might help Brad leave the classroom feeling a little less upset and make it easier for you to get him out if he could have two or three minutes to finish what he is doing when you arrive. I'd be happy to have Brad's backpack and coat at the table with him to expedite getting him out the door. Having those couple of minutes to transition would probably help Brad feel calmer and would make your walk to the car a lot more pleasant. Would you be willing to consider this possibility?"

By honoring the mother's need for control and her wish to be a firm authority figure, Mr. Conrad does not make her feel defensive or argumentative. It is easy for Mrs. Parker to agree to his suggestion, since it offers a way to make things easier for everyone. Mrs. Parker agrees to give it a try, and the next afternoon the teacher explains the new plan to Brad. The transition from school to home is easier for Brad, and Mr. Conrad is able to talk a little bit about Brad's day with his mother as well. Mrs. Parker feels more connected to Brad's experiences at school.

It can be difficult to find something positive to say to a parent whose behavior is frustrating. Being strategic in acknowledging a parent's positive characteristics or intentions will enable the parent to consider joining with the teacher to create a better outcome for the child at school. Often, even after finding the positive statement to say to the family member, teachers have the strong urge to add, "but when you do that, you . . ." or words to that effect. When a family member hears the word *but*, she is very likely to become defensive in anticipation of the coming criticism. Avoid qualifying your positive statements when you use this strategy. It may take a little practice to perfect this approach, but it is quite helpful in many difficult situations with families. Try practicing with your fellow staff members before trying it out with families. Once perfected, it has the potential to help teachers overcome many challenging situations and remove roadblocks to successful family-teacher partnerships.

Embarking on the path toward partnership with families is an act of courage. It requires a high level of professionalism and a mature recognition of the hugely important role of families. The benefits that teachers reap from establishing ongoing, respectful relationships with parents far outweigh the challenges involved in creating them. Parents who feel understood, valued, and heard by their children's teachers are significantly more likely to engage in activities at school, provide the support that children need to be successful, and connect personally in ways that are helpful and constructive.

Questions for Reflection

1. What are your strengths in working with families?
2. What do you find most challenging about working with families?
3. What strategies have you found to be the most helpful in building positive connections with parents?
4. After reading this chapter and reflecting on your work with families, what is one area where you could make a change?
5. What specific steps would you need to take to make progress in this area?
6. Think of a specific family member you find challenging in some way. What components of this chapter can help you develop a more positive working relationship with that person?
7. If you feel it is appropriate, edit your list of goals and values that you created in Chapter One.

Supporting Development of Social-Emotional Skills

Preschool children are beginning to explore the wider world, developing relationships with people outside their immediate families, learning how to interact with peers, and making decisions as they test boundaries and explore their environment. Most of young children's learning occurs through experiential activities during play.

Developmentally appropriate expectations for this age group include an understanding that they are learning self-regulation—the ability to manage and modulate their feelings and behavior. Part of self-regulation is learning the vocabulary to express emotions, preferences, and needs. Teachers understand that children need to learn how to use language to solve problems rather than resorting to physical aggression. When asked to set goals for the children in their classrooms, teachers often give a list such as the following:

- To control their impulses and develop self-regulation skills
- To express their feelings clearly
- To learn to cooperate with others
- To develop the ability to negotiate in play situations
- To learn how to problem solve and engage in conflict resolution without resorting to physical aggression

These are important and reasonable goals for preschoolers, and to accomplish each one, teachers must provide guidance.

79

Using Impulse Control and Developing Vocabulary

What skills do children need to have before they can learn to use words to resolve conflict and negotiate peer relationships? First, children must develop impulse control. They must be able to contain their feelings long enough to think about using language. Second, they must have the ability to translate their feelings into words rather than deeds. As adults, we take such skills for granted. For young children, however, this is actually a pretty tall order.

"Use your words!" is a common expression one hears in early childhood classrooms. Although the underlying sentiment is appropriate, this particular expression is often poorly understood by children. In many cases, the child does not know which words to use, so hearing a teacher demand that she use words to express her feelings or respond to a frustration in the classroom is not particularly helpful. When teachers reflect on the steps necessary for children to learn the skills to negotiate conflict, they are better equipped to provide the coaching and guidance that children need.

The child's ability to use language appropriately is affected by her overall developmental level, her level of language acquisition and expressive capacity, and her family background. When teachers recognize and reflect on the variety of skill levels among the children in their classroom, they are better prepared to develop the kinds of strategies and levels of intervention they will need to support the children in using words more frequently and effectively.

Children begin to use words in navigating interactions with peers sometime between the ages of two and three, assuming they are in situations in which they are exposed to other children on a regular basis, such as at home with siblings, in play groups, or in group care settings.

The words toddlers use are often territorial, such as "Mine!" or "No!" Gradually their language use expands to include phrases such as "Don't do that!" or "I want it!" or "Give it to me!" or "My turn!"

Using words and phrases in a more sophisticated way with peers does not usually begin for most children until around three years of age. By that age, many children have good language development and emerging impulse control. Recognizing that such skills are a prerequisite to using words can help us understand why so many children struggle to negotiate conflict successfully. Some children may be developmentally delayed, at risk, or under stress for a variety of reasons. Some enter preschool programs with poor language development and especially poor impulse control. What are appropriate expectations for such children? For all young preschoolers, teachers must help them manage interactions when conflict occurs, setting clear limits and acting as models. For children with limited language and impulse control, the teacher must be even more directly involved.

Three-year-old Lisa hits Joshua, who is drawing with markers at a table and refuses to share any of them with her. The teacher walks over to Lisa and says, "No hitting, Lisa. That hurts," and then adds, "It looks like you wanted some markers, but those are the ones Joshua is using. Let's get you some markers from the bin on the shelf. It can be frustrating if you don't get what you want when you want it. There are enough markers here for children who need them."

To help Lisa with this situation, the teacher had to be watching the play in the classroom carefully and noticing when incidents occur. The teacher also could model a way for Joshua to resolve the conflict with Lisa: "I'm using these. There's more in the bin on the shelf; you can take some there." Although a three-year-old may be unlikely to use sophisticated language to resolve conflict, modeling desired behavior can help a child learn an alternative to an aggressive response.

To use words to express feelings and navigate social interactions, children need sufficient language development to be able to think of the words that describe their feelings. Generally, most preschoolers are familiar with three basic feeling words: *mad, sad,* and *happy*. Human emotions, however, do not always fit neatly into these categories.

Kaitlyn is playing with playdough, attempting to roll it into a ball. She has seen a friend roll playdough into a ball, and she wants to do the same thing. Try as she might, however, her ball looks nothing like her friend's. After working with the playdough for a while, Kaitlyn throws it on the floor. Noticing her action, her teacher walks over and gently says, "Oh my goodness, Kaitlyn! It is so frustrating when you try to do something and it just doesn't come out the way you want it to! You look really frustrated with your playdough. Maybe we can work together, and I can help you learn a way to roll it that might work a little better for you. Would you like to try?"

With this simple exchange, Kaitlyn's teacher is doing a number of things:

- **She is recognizing and validating the child's feelings.** She describes what she sees happening and validates Kaitlyn's feelings about the playdough not looking the way she wanted it to look. She is not judging, just acknowledging Kaitlyn's behavioral response.
- **She is introducing new vocabulary.** She introduces the words *frustrated* and *frustrating* to Kaitlyn, giving her a way to describe her feelings.
- **She is offering a productive response.** She offers to teach Kaitlyn a new strategy for making a playdough ball that might have a rounder shape.

The child will get the help she needs to be more proficient with playdough, and she has learned a new word to describe a feeling that she may have perceived simply as anger. When teachers invest time and energy into teaching a wide range of words that describe feelings, children become more able to manage their feelings because they can express them and get help with them.

There are many resources available to help children learn about feelings. Vanderbilt University sponsors the Center on the Social and Emotional Foundations for Early Learning, which offers some wonderful tool kits, materials, a bibliography of children's stories that deal with different feelings, and downloadable feelings charts that teachers can use with children. Using high-quality children's literature is a wonderful way to teach children about feelings in a nonthreatening way, as they connect with the characters in the stories. The stories serve as springboards to talk about feelings that the children experience.

Young children's brains are not yet developed in such a way that they can think, reflect, and express the impact of their experiences on their

The Insightful Teacher

feelings. Nor can they predict or understand the connection between those inner feelings and their behavior. Through teachers' careful observations of children and regular communication with families, they can learn how children express their feelings through their behavior, and they can help children understand themselves better. Be a keen observer and look for teachable moments—opportunities to identify and label a child's feelings while helping him manage them successfully. Through these real-life experiences, children will recognize a broad range of emotions. It is not always obvious what feeling underlies a specific behavior; learn to recognize the feelings that children are experiencing and expressing.

Amaya comes to school one morning in a particularly grumpy mood. Her teacher, who is very sensitive to separation concerns, notices that Amaya's mom seems particularly hurried as she says goodbye to Amaya.

Despite her lack of effort at engaging with them, Amaya pouts and complains that her friends will not play with her. Her teacher says, "Looks like you're having a bit of a hard morning today. Sometimes when children are feeling sad or upset or are missing their moms, they might act kind of grumpy at school. Do you think you might be feeling that way today?"

Amaya begins to cry. "Mommy pushed me into school today!" Her teacher takes Amaya onto her lap and comforts her. When Amaya is feeling a little better, her teacher offers to let Amaya dictate a note to Mom about how she is feeling. After putting the note in Amaya's cubby, her teacher helps Amaya rejoin her friends to play.

The teacher has many choices in how to respond to Amaya's behavior. She does not tell Amaya how she is feeling. Instead, she offers Amaya reassurance by letting her know that many other children might act in similar ways if they are feeling upset or sad or are missing their moms. Had she tried to pronounce the reason for Amaya's behavior, rather than letting Amaya confirm the cause, she could have been wrong in her assessment.

Not all children will respond as Amaya did and confide in their teacher immediately. Some might not be ready to acknowledge their feelings. Even if this is the case, it is still good that the teacher makes the attempt. The teacher can always follow up, saying, "It's okay if you don't want to talk about how you are feeling right now. Sometimes that's hard. Let's figure out how I can help you have a better day today." Having opened the door for the child to communicate about her feelings, the teacher has introduced the concept that there is a connection between feelings and behavior. This understanding is an important element in developing a child's ability to reflect.

Cooperating with Peers

Children learn through play. Through their interactions with peers, children learn how to communicate needs and preferences, how to cooperate with others, and how to accept differences. As much as possible, let play continue uninterrupted, and allow children to develop their ability to cooperate. However, instances will arise when a teacher's guidance will help keep the play flowing smoothly. If you notice a play situation heading in the direction of conflict, simply adding another element can distract the children and set them back on course, allowing play to continue.

Carly and LaVon are playing with a barn and some farm animals. Carly has the horse, and LaVon has the sheep. LaVon says that he wants to play with the horse, and Carly says that she wants to keep it. Before the situation escalates, the teacher moves in and says, "Oh my goodness! Do you see that mama pig and her babies over there? They are so hungry, and they can't find any food! Could somebody bring the food trough over to them so that they can get something to eat?"

Carly immediately responds, "I will get their food!" She places the food trough near the pigs and begins playing with them, enabling LaVon to play with the horse.

Often, simply by entering into the children's play and adding a new play element, a teacher can avert a potential conflict altogether. This is a creative option to support and maintain high-quality, productive play.

Of course, occasionally you will need to intervene in play to keep everyone safe. Use safety interventions as opportunities to help children understand the link between their actions and the consequences for themselves and others.

The teachers have created a bicycle route, allowing the children to ride on a sidewalk that curves around the outer border of the playground. They have established some rules, including the requirement that the children ride in one direction only.

Michael loves going as fast as he can on his bicycle. He does not always abide by the one-way guideline, and one afternoon he rides directly into another child's bicycle. Sean, the other rider, bursts into tears after scraping his arm on the cement bike path. The teacher, Joanna, takes Sean inside to give him first aid. Meanwhile, Michael rides off unharmed.

When Joanna returns with Sean, she calls Michael over and talks with the boys. "Well, Michael, I know you love to ride your bicycle fast, and that sometimes you go the wrong way down our one-way bike path. Today that caused Sean to get hurt. Do you see his bandage? He was hurt and afraid when you knocked into him, and he scraped his arm. Is there anything you might want to do to help him feel better?"

Michael replies, "Sorry, Sean! But you were in my way!"

The teacher asks if there was anything Sean wants to say to Michael about what happened. Sean responds, "Don't bump into me, Michael!"

Joanna thanks Sean for telling Michael how he feels and sends him on his way. She turns to Michael and says, "We need to figure out a way that you can ride a bicycle more safely so that children don't get hurt. Do you have any ideas about this?"

Michael says, "I like to go really fast!"

Joanna responds, "Yes, I know you do. And you have pretty good balance on the bicycle, too! But it's really important to go only one way and not to go too fast when there is too much traffic on the bike path. It's kind of like when you're in a car with Mom or Dad and they can't drive very fast because there are a lot of other cars on the road."

Michael insists, "But, I'm a fast driver!"

His teacher replies, "You are a fast driver, but sometimes children can get hurt when you drive fast. Maybe I could make a sign to hold up when there's traffic and you have to drive slowly. When you see the sign, you need to slow down. Could that work for you?" Michael nods.

If a child gets hurt because of another child's action, a teacher often will restrict the offending child's involvement in the activity that caused the harm. Young children typically cannot anticipate the consequences of their actions. There are a few things to note in this example. First, when Joanna asks Michael if there is something he could do to help Sean feel better, he apologizes. However, if Michael had not apologized, that also would be an acceptable outcome. The goal is to help Michael understand that he can do something to make amends for causing harm and that his teacher would support this choice. Offering a child the option to do something that might help a peer feel better, rather than forcing an apology, supports the idea that making amends is a good thing to do. Second, Joanna praises Michael's fast riding when he seems to focus on that issue. She validates his skill before proceeding to the problem-solving piece. Third, after she and Michael agree on a plan to help him be safer on the bicycles, she allows him to return to riding. She does not deprive him of his favorite activity in an attempt to help him learn how to be safer.

So much social and emotional learning occurs during play. Often, children will notice differences as they play together. When a child is trying to learn a skill such as pumping his legs on the swing, for example, another child may comment, "You don't know how to swing like I do!" This is an opportunity for the teacher to observe, "Look at those legs! They are pushing out hard and then you are really working on getting them back under you so that you can swing higher all by yourself. Learning to pump that way on the swing is tough, and you are really working on learning how to do it. You must feel good about that!" By acknowledging the child's efforts as he attempts to master a new skill and noting that the work is difficult, she is modeling accepting differences. The idea here is not to directly compare children as they are engaged in the same activity but to notice individually what skills they have mastered. The children's play can continue uninterrupted, but the child can feel that his efforts are acknowledged.

Negotiating Play and Navigating Conflicts

When children are first learning to navigate conflicts with peers, it can be helpful to offer a specific phrase they can use when something is not working well for them. A program I was involved with chose the phrase "I don't like that!" It let the other child know that the child with whom she was playing was not pleased; however, it was not guaranteed to have an impact on the play partner. The peer may not care that her friend does not like that. The beauty of such a phrase is that not only does it give children a beginning step toward managing difficult interactions, but also it alerts the teacher to a potential conflict.

Four-year-olds Josh and Stephen are building with the large wooden blocks. From the art table, the teacher hears Josh yell, "I don't like that, Stephen!" His ears perk up and he looks over to see an argument starting over which blocks will be placed where and who will be in charge of the play. He walks over and asks, "Hi guys! What's happening here?"

Josh responds, "We agreed to build an office so we could go to work, and I started building this tower, but Stephen keeps taking the blocks away!"

Stephen pipes up, "But, he's using all the long blocks, and I need some for our car!"

The teacher replies, "So, Josh, you were working on the office tower that you and Stephen agreed to build, but then Stephen took away the blocks you were using." Then he gives equal attention to Stephen's side of the story, saying, "Stephen, you didn't like that Josh was using the long blocks you needed to build the car." The children nod.

The teacher then asks, "How do you guys think you could solve this problem in a way that you can both feel okay? Josh is trying to build the office tower, and Stephen is building the car. You need both for your play idea."

Josh says, "Maybe we could split up the long blocks and put some of the square ones together for the other side!" Stephen quickly agrees.

The technique their teacher uses with Josh and Stephen is a version of what I call the Validate, Suggest, Depart, Acknowledge approach to conflict resolution. There are a handful of similar intervention strategies designed by various early childhood professionals and psychologists to help children learn how to resolve conflicts peacefully. They all involve a multistep process in which the teacher moves into the situation and works with the children, then moves back out so that they can experience some problem-solving efforts on their own. By moving in, the teacher helps the children learn how to get past the feelings that are interfering with their ability to think about solutions.

- **Validate:** This approach includes the act of validating each child's perception of the incident or conflict. In the example, the teacher repeats what each child reports to him, without judgment and without interruptions or comments from the other child. The teacher just notes Josh's experience as reported to him, then gives equal attention to Stephen's side of the story.
- **Suggest:** After validating each child's version of events, the teacher then suggests to both boys that they might be able to think of a solution to the problem. This sends the message that the teacher has confidence in the boys' ability to come up with new ideas.

- **Depart:** At this point, the teacher gives the boys a few minutes to discuss the situation. The teacher may choose to actually physically depart or to simply sit quietly while the children problem solve. His choice will depend on his assessment of the children's ability to work together independently. Some children may need the teacher to remain present or even to suggest some possible solutions if the children are at a loss. It is essential, however, to give the children an opportunity to talk about the problem and come up with their own ideas first, before the teacher adds his thoughts or ideas.

- **Acknowledge:** The last piece of the process is the teacher's return to find out what the boys came up with. He listens, offers support and acknowledges their solution, and sends them on their way.

Although keeping play running smoothly is optimal, sometimes children's play must be interrupted when the children are displaying inappropriate behavior.

Tashwan and Max are playing together in the sandbox, and Sophie is playing nearby. Sophie yells, "Stop throwing sand!" at the boys.

The teacher hears her and walks over to the sandbox. "What seems to be the problem?" Sophie says, "I'm trying to build a castle, and Tashwan and Max are throwing sand and I'm getting all messed up!" The teacher notices that Sophie does, indeed, have some sand on her hair and body.

She has a choice. There is a rule at the school that throwing sand is not allowed. She could tell Tashwan and Max that they have broken this rule and require them to leave the sandbox and go play somewhere else. Instead, she asks the boys, "What's up with the sand, guys? Sophie has sand in her hair and on her clothes. See?"

Tashwan explains, "We weren't throwing. We're just digging and sometimes it gets messy! Sophie needs to get out of our way!"

The teacher sizes up the situation and sees that the children are a bit physically close to one another. She draws a line in the sand with her finger, saying, "You are playing really close to each other. Here's the boundary line. You guys need to stay over here on this side, and, Sophie, you can have the space on this side. If you don't get so close to each other, we can avoid the problem of messy sand. Can you handle the plan?" The children agree, and the play continues.

The teacher chooses not to focus on the fact that a rule was being broken. Rather, she focuses on allowing the children's play to continue. Rules are suggestions created to keep children safe and to help promote and maintain productive play situations. If a rule is broken for some reason, the first question should be, "How can this problem be addressed in a way that will allow the play to continue?" Sometimes teachers can get caught up in the rule or guideline itself and forget about the goal behind the rule.

Experiencing the consequences of one's behavior can mean that a teacher insists that a child look at his peer's facial expression and recognize that his words or actions have caused pain or distress. In the sandbox example, having the boys recognize that, intentional or not, their actions did lead to Sophie having sand all over her body and being uncomfortable is a consequence. They then learn a way to adjust their actions. A consequence does not have to be deprivation or punishment; children can learn to take responsibility for their actions and to behave in more positive ways with their teacher's help.

Another useful strategy for addressing conflict is to incorporate the element of surprise into one's interventions. When teachers have a repertoire of responses to children's behavior and occasionally respond in a way that is not entirely predictable, this captures the children's attention. All interventions should arise out of the same philosophical approach and incorporate the same essential messages and lessons, but delivering them in new and different ways can make life in the classroom more interesting for everyone.

One example of such a potentially surprising intervention is to respond only to the victim when there has been some form of physical aggression.

Sally pushes DaJonna as they disagree over which doll each girl will play with. Instead of approaching Sally to talk with her about pushing, the teacher chooses to approach DaJonna. "Oh my goodness! Your arm must hurt. Can I look at it? It looks a little red. Let me massage it a little bit. Do you need a bandage? I'm so sorry that happened to you! Sally really needs to work on using words to say how she feels instead of using her hands to push!"

At this point, Sally will most likely be quite surprised at being ignored; although, she certainly has heard every word the teacher has said to DaJonna. DaJonna feels better at having been attended to, and the teacher has made it clear that pushing is never an acceptable way to resolve conflicts.

Most children lash out physically when they feel overwhelmed by their impulses and are not capable of figuring out alternatives. In such cases, the physical aggression is in response to a specific situation and is targeted to a specific person. Therefore, if the teacher chooses to ignore the aggressor occasionally and focuses her attention on the victim, the aggressor likely will move away and cause no further harm. Occasionally, however, there may be a child in a classroom who lashes out aggressively not once, but serially. For such a child, this creative strategy of ignoring the aggressor and attending only to the victim would not be appropriate, because other children could be at risk. In such a case, the aggressor must be attended to immediately, to help her calm down and to protect other potential victims.

Another surprising intervention is in response to a conflict over who can be the mother during dramatic play at outdoor time. A common response to this type of impasse is to make the children separate and play somewhere else. However, that solution does not resolve the problem.

LaKeisha, who is four years old, and Susanna, who is three and a half, are playing in and around a playhouse with some other children. LaKeisha insists that Susanna must be the little sister, but Susanna wants to be the mother. Both girls are quite frustrated and are holding their ground as their voices rise. Their teacher, Stephanie, approaches the girls to help them resolve their conflict. "I hear some yelling over here, girls. What's happening?" Both girls begin talking at once, and Stephanie says, "Hold on, hold on! I want to hear both of you. One person at a time. LaKeisha, tell me your idea of what's happening and what the problem is."

LaKeisha says, "I wanted to play house and Susanna wanted to play, too, and I told her I was the mother and she could be the little sister, but she won't and she's yelling!"

Her teacher says, "So, you had the idea to play house out here, and Susanna wanted to play, too. But, when you told her you would be the mother, she refused to be the little sister and started yelling." Then, Stephanie asks Susanna her idea about happened.

Susanna responds, "I hate being the little sister! I never get to be the mother, and LaKeisha won't let me play!"

Stephanie repeats, "So, you don't like being the little sister, and you feel like LaKeisha won't let you play house the way you want to. You know, families come in all shapes and sizes; sometimes there is a grandma who lives in the family, sometimes the mommy and her grown-up sister live together and take care of the children, or sometimes two people who are neighbors like to do baking projects together at each other's houses. I'll bet you two could figure out a way that you can both have a good time playing house together. I'll give you a couple of minutes to talk about it." She departs briefly.

By describing a variety of different possibilities for family constellations and how different adults might end up being together in the same house, Stephanie offers some ideas regarding how the girls might resolve their particular conflict. But, she states the ideas in a general way so the girls have room to improvise on their own. A few minutes later, when she returns, the girls have decided to be cousins and are baking brownies for all of their "children." Their teacher says, "Brilliant! I hope you'll invite me for brownies, too! I love brownies!"

When children believe that their feelings and perceptions are understood and validated, they are much more willing to move forward and not stay stuck in rigid positions. A critical element of this process is the fact that the teacher is not searching for the guilty party. Rather, her goal is to help both parties work together to find a solution. This shift from assigning blame to enabling children to resolve conflict and return to play is very powerful. It frees adults from the role of enforcer to the role of facilitator and support figure.

Building Community

Through communicating a positive spin on listening to others' ideas and on the process of learning, the teacher lays the groundwork for building community and acceptance in the classroom. When children can see individual perspectives and differences in a noncompetitive and nonjudgmental way, they are more likely to be understanding of one another. This approach sets a model for tolerance, patience, and inclusion, skills that will prepare young children for success as they progress through later school experiences. As children develop their problem-solving skills, teachers can use strategies such as the following to further strengthen these skills and build a classroom community.

- Peace table
- Classroom meetings
- Children's books
- Positive leadership
- Focused curriculum units
- Storytelling, dramatization, and class books

Peace Table

For children who are familiar with the four-step conflict resolution process and are becoming more competent problem solvers, a classroom table designated as a peace table can be a good resource. The idea is that the teacher identifies a special place where two or three children can sit and talk about ways to resolve a conflict. Instead of the teacher going through the conflict-resolution process with the children, she can suggest that the children talk at the peace table. This is a resource to be used by children who already have developed strong problem-solving skills and may be ready to have such discussions on their own. Children whose problem-solving and resolution skills are not as strong likely will need support from the teacher.

If the children at the table seem to be struggling to find a solution to their dilemma, the teacher may offer additional assistance as needed. By recognizing the children's skills, the teacher is supporting their ability to work through conflicts on their own, without the need of her direct involvement.

Classroom Meetings

When there is a pattern of behavior in a classroom that involves more than one or two children, classroom meetings are an excellent strategy for engaging the children in group problem solving. When children play an active part in the process, they will feel more committed to the solution.

A classroom meeting uses the same setup as circle time. To begin the meeting, the teacher announces what the focus will be: "I've been thinking a lot about clean-up time. What I see is toys, markers, and puzzle pieces left on the floor; doll clothes thrown into pretend food drawers in the dramatic play area; and books left open on the floor where they can get torn or stepped on. We need to figure out a way to do a more careful and thorough job of cleaning up so that our toys will be in good repair and no one gets hurt from tripping over things left on the floor. Does anyone have an idea about how we can do a better job at clean-up time?"

The idea here is that the discussion then becomes a brainstorming session. Essentially, any idea a child might have is an acceptable possibility. The teacher acts as the scribe and writes down or illustrates the ideas so that all the children can see them. A child might call out, "The girls should do all the cleanup!" followed by laughter. The teacher would dutifully record this idea without comment or judgment.

When a number of ideas are listed and all voices have been heard, the teacher ends the discussion phase and begins to narrow the choices. The teacher, being the adult, gets veto power over suggestions that are inappropriate or unfair. He might say, "I can understand why the boys might like it if the girls did all the cleanup, but then it wouldn't really be fair for the boys to get to play with the toys if they hadn't participated in cleaning them up. I will draw a line through that one."

This is the point when the teacher's creativity must really shine. He must find one of the remaining ideas that contains a kernel of possibility. Then he can add his own suggestions to the idea, expressed in such a way that he is extending or enhancing the idea the children have suggested. It might look something like this: "Sean suggested that everybody put away at least three things. Then, everybody could look around and check to see that everything is cleaned up. If someone finds something, he will pick it up so that his group can move on to getting ready for outdoor time. How does that sound?" Focusing on what happens after children comply with adult directives is an effective strategy for engaging cooperation. Once the group agrees, the teacher can draw a simple picture of the plan, perhaps of a child picking up some toys, and post it on a wall in the classroom. The teacher will remind children of the plan when it is clean-up time, emphasizing that it is the solution that the children chose and reinforcing what a good job they did in coming up with such a workable idea.

Encouraging children to think of ideas that improve classroom life promotes growth. Supporting children in speaking up and finding potential solutions, demonstrating respect for their ideas, and implementing them all build a sense of community and shared responsibility.

Children's Books

High-quality children's literature can be a wonderful tool for communicating and supporting classroom guidelines. Reading stories on topics that are relevant to ongoing concerns in classrooms can be a helpful way to stimulate nonthreatening discussions of behaviors about which teachers are concerned.

When children show teasing or bullying behaviors, for example, teachers can read a story about that topic and use it as a springboard for conversation. Choose such books carefully; not all topical books send the right message. Some use humor, which is great, but if the solution proposed in the story is for the victim of teasing or bullying to simply turn the tables on the bully, that may not be the message the teacher wants to convey. Look for stories that teach children strategies for getting help when they are being hurt by others. Discuss issues in the context of a story, letting the children identify with characters rather than having to talk strictly about themselves. This can open up a discussion that can then move toward a more personal conversation that is relevant to what is happening in the classroom.

A program at which I was a consultant often used the book *Bailey the Big Bully* by Lizi Boyd to discuss the topic of teasing and bullying. In the story, Bailey is hit on the nose. Nicholas, a boy who sometimes teased the younger children in the classroom, spoke up in defense of Bailey, saying that it is not fair that Bailey is hit. Other children disagreed and said that Bailey deserved it for being mean to the kids in the neighborhood.

The teacher asked, "Does anyone in our school ever feel like some of the children on Bailey's block?" And a few children said that they did and described that they did not like it when Nicholas teased them. Problem solving that focuses on one child as the aggressor must be handled very delicately. The teacher responded, "When teasing happens, what can someone do to help that person feel better?"

A child piped up, "Tell a teacher!" That led to a discussion about what kind of "tattling" is helpful and what is not so helpful. If a child tells the teacher something has happened that needs attending to, such as a child getting hurt or needing help, this is helpful. If a child simply reports on other children who may have taken someone else's toy, this is not helpful because it is not up to any child to resolve other children's possible conflicts or to enforce the classroom rules.

As the discussion continued, the teacher reassured the children, "Nicholas is working on using kinder words and gentle hands with the younger children. That is something I will continue to help him with. If you hear him saying or doing something unkind, perhaps you can gently remind him that we are kind at our school. We all need to remember that our words can hurt people's feelings sometimes, and bullying words or actions are never okay." By generalizing to all of the children, the teacher shifted the focus off of Nicholas to avoid scapegoating him.

The teacher created a poster listing the positive behaviors that she and the children want in their classroom: "In our classroom, we use kind words and gentle hands, and we welcome all who want to play with us." She added pictures to represent these behaviors, so the children could connect the images with the words.

Leo the Late Bloomer by Robert Kraus is another children's book that can facilitate discussion. It is the story of a baby lion who is somewhat slow in gaining the skills that the other lions have already learned. His parents worry that there is something wrong with him, but one day he just figures it out and blooms. This story is an excellent springboard for a discussion with children about how some things come easier to some of us than to others. We all have strengths and challenges. The concept of "working on" skills and abilities helps children understand and accept differences they notice in others. When a teacher says, for example, "Wow, you are really working on throwing the ball into the basket. Practicing is how children learn," she is reinforcing the idea that skills are acquired gradually. This way of talking about children's varying skill levels decreases competition in the classroom and builds acceptance and a feeling of community.

Positive Leadership

As children develop their social skills through play with their peers, they experiment with power, inclusion, and exclusion. Often, this experimentation takes the form of teasing. Four- and five-year-olds, whose language skills are quite sophisticated and who are engaged in developing social relationships with peers, are just beginning to figure out that having a number of friends and playing with peers does not mean being disloyal to a special friend. Children this age may make comments such as, "You can't play with me today because you're not my best friend!" or "You can't come to my birthday party!" or even "You aren't wearing purple, so you can't play with us today!"

It is important for teachers to intervene with such exclusionary behavior. This dynamic is an emergent form of bullying that needs to be nipped in the bud. Children who initiate these behaviors actually do have some leadership skills, but teachers must help them turn those skills into more positive leadership behaviors.

Tamara is a popular four-and-a-half-year-old girl. She is close friends with a few other girls in the class, and they have occasional play dates outside of school. One day, Tamara notices that she and her buddies are all wearing leggings. She suggests that they make a rule that only children wearing leggings can play with them in the dramatic play area. Susanna, who is wearing a dress, wants to play with them, but Tamara quickly warns, "You can't come in here to play because you're not wearing leggings!" The other two girls agree, "Yeah, that's our rule!" The excluded child walks away, forlorn.

The teacher sees Susanna's expression and asks her what's wrong. When she learns what has happened, she goes over to the area where Tamara is ruling the roost. She asks, "What's up with the leggings rule, girls?" Tamara explains. The teacher listens then responds, "Tamara, you have some great ideas for fantasy play. I love how you came up with the idea of a restaurant with waitresses in uniforms. That's really creative, and it's clear you girls are having fun. However, in this classroom we don't exclude children who want to join into play. That hurts feelings. Besides, it looks to me like you have too many waitresses and no customers at this restaurant! I bet Susanna would love to be a customer and order something good to eat!" The girls agree, and Susanna is delighted to be included.

Had Susanna wanted to be a waitress, too, the teacher would have had to work with the girls to figure out a way to include her. But, this intervention was sufficient. The teacher validated Tamara's creativity and leadership skills before she moved into pointing out the hurt caused by excluding Susanna. She gave Tamara a way to use her leadership skills positively. Children need to learn that being a leader does not necessarily mean excluding others or creating rigid hierarchies. While not everyone in the classroom needs to be a friend, everyone must be treated with kindness and accepted into play situations.

Focused Curriculum Units

Another program I worked with decided to focus on the concept of kindness. The teachers had noticed some difficult behaviors and attitudes among the children and developed a curriculum unit to address those behaviors. They read books about friendship, taught vocabulary about cooperation, and played games in which children had to work together to succeed. In addition, they built a kindness tree in the classroom—a stuffed paper tree trunk pinned to a large bulletin board. Each time a teacher saw a child displaying kindness, she would write it down on a sticky note and put it on the tree as a leaf. Families loved coming in at pickup time to look at the tree and see whether their children had earned leaves that day. The teachers let the families bring in examples of their children being kind at home, as well.

The whole tenor of the classroom changed, and the children looked for ways to help one another and demonstrate kindness. The curriculum expanded to include generosity, patience, respect, and caring for others who are less fortunate. It became one of the most beloved curriculum units the program had ever developed.

Storytelling, Dramatization, and Class Books

Other strategies that build community include shared storytelling, story dictation and dramatization, and making class books. Shared storytelling can be done in any size group, but it may be easier in small groups so that children do not have to wait long to contribute to the story. The teacher introduces a topic that the children are interested in, such as a story the children have heard and find very appealing, a special event at school, a topic of study, or something the children did outdoors. The teacher begins the story, and the children continue it. For example, the teacher might say, "Once upon a time, some children decided to make a snowman outside. The snow was pretty wet and good for rolling, so Sam began to roll a snowball and make it bigger. Then what happened, Courtney?" Courtney continues, "It got bigger, but then Alison fell on it, and Sam got mad!" Each child adds to the story in turn.

To make a class book, the teacher writes down what each child says on a separate page. When the story is complete, each child illustrates her part of the tale. The children choose a title, then the teacher laminates the pages and binds the newly created book. Such books can become beloved symbols of classroom community.

Vivian Paley, a noted author and early childhood education researcher, developed the technique of story dictation and dramatization, in which the teacher writes down verbatim what each child says. She asks questions to encourage the children to add details to their narratives; for example, if a child says, "There was a flower," then the teacher can ask about the flower's color, location, and scent and ask what happens to the flower. She can encourage the children to then act out the story. These stories are quite entertaining to act out and can be highly motivating and helpful for children who do not have strong verbal skills.

In a classroom in which I volunteered, I noticed a quiet five-year-old boy. I often used story dictation with the children, but this child never approached me to participate. After I had been in the classroom for a number of weeks, I encouraged him to come over and try it.

At first, his stories consisted of one sentence such as, "There was a rainbow." I dutifully wrote down his words, and he was quite pleased. Over time, he saw that some of the more verbally advanced children were dictating long stories, and he seemed interested. I asked him lots of questions to help him elaborate: "How did the rainbow get there? Did it rain earlier? Tell me what happened before the rainbow was in the sky. Oh, I love seeing rainbows! Was there anyone there to look at this rainbow? Was it a person or an animal?" Gradually, he began to enlarge his stories and, by springtime, he, too, dictated a story that took up more than a page. His smile was as big as the large lined paper I wrote on, and we were both totally delighted! He acted out his story for the class, and the children clapped, recognizing that this child had made significant progress. Their enthusiasm and kindness moved all of us. Talk about community building!

There are many ways to teach children to use words. Our focus as educators and supportive adults is to enable them to recognize and name their feelings, manage their emotions, get along with others, and feel a part of a classroom community in which everyone is valued and understood. This experience will follow them as they move through their educational experience and will equip them to be successful interpersonally as well as academically.

Questions for Reflection

1. Reflect on your expectations of young children to use their words. Does thinking about the skills children need to be able to do this affect your expectations? If so, how? If not, why not?

2. What is your reaction to the concept of planning interventions with children that enable play to continue, rather than interrupting play to address behavior? If you have a different perspective, how do you see things differently?

3. Think about Michael, the racing child who collided with another child on the bike path. What did you think of the teacher's intervention with him? Is there a child in your classroom who might benefit from a similar approach? What would that intervention look like?

4. What are your thoughts about validating children's feelings as you help them learn to resolve conflicts with others? Have you ever been in a situation as an adult in which someone's understanding of your perceptions, experience, or feelings was helpful to you as you tried to resolve a conflict?

5. Which strategy in this chapter appeals to you the most? How might you use it in your classroom?

6. If you feel it is appropriate, edit your list of goals and values that you created in Chapter One.

Redefining Fairness and Focusing on Goals

Many people believe that *fairness* means that every person should be treated in the same way. After all, they reason, if people are treated differently, that must mean there is discrimination and unfairness. This definition often leads teachers to focus on using consequences and punishment to manage inappropriate behaviors in the classroom. I define fairness differently: *Fairness* means that everyone has an equal right to have his needs met.

My definition of fairness implies that people's needs are not always the same. In a classroom, children come with different experiences, skill levels, and cultural values. Meeting the needs of an individual child may mean making exceptions to a rule or having different expectations, for different children. Of course, teachers need to have safety rules and a basic, predictable schedule, as well as a variety of group expectations to have a productive classroom. At the same time, however, it may be necessary to make exceptions to some of these expectations for certain children in certain situations. Figuring out when and how to make such exceptions is a key component of effective, supportive, reflective teaching.

A useful technique for considering how to respond to challenging behaviors is to keep in mind one's goals for young children. What do you want the children to learn and achieve during the preschool years? When I ask this at my workshops, some of the common responses I receive include the following:

- Self-control
- Cooperation
- Social skills
- Joy in learning
- Pre-academic skills
- Self-confidence

I do not get responses such as suffering, humiliation, or guilt and shame; yet, these are the feelings that children typically experience when assigned consequences or punishment. In *Counterpoint*, a publication of the National Association of State Directors of Special Education, NASDSE president John Herner observed:

> If a child doesn't know how to read, we teach.
> If a child doesn't know how to swim, we teach.
> If a child doesn't know how to multiply, we teach.
> If a child doesn't know how to drive, we teach.
> If a child doesn't know how to behave, we... teach? punish?
> Why can't we finish the last sentence as automatically as we do the others?

It is our job, as teachers of young children, to teach appropriate behavior.

Because young children often lack the vocabulary to describe and express their emotions, they express feelings through their behavior. They are impulsive, and although preschoolers are learning self-control, it certainly is not a skill they have mastered. Even a child who has a high level of verbal skill may not be able to control her impulses when she is angry, frightened, hurt, or frustrated. Understanding the words for things does not automatically translate into the ability to put those words into action.

It is essential that teachers be keen observers of children's behavior. They need to see the context in which children exhibit what author Dan Gartrell calls *mistaken behavior*. In using this term, he emphasizes the fact that young children still are learning how to behave properly. Viewed in this light, it is easier to see challenging behaviors as less deliberate. Understanding the context of such behaviors will enable the teacher to understand better what feeling the child may have been expressing through his actions, and thus will offer clues to helping the child resolve the problem he is experiencing. Look at difficult behaviors as problems to be solved. Help children learn, gain self-esteem and confidence, and improve their behavior, all at the same time.

The teacher has a long-standing rule that each child sits on a label with the child's name on it on the rug during circle time. Four-year-old Samantha announces that she does not want to sit on her label on the rug.

What should the teacher's response be? When I present this situation to teachers in my workshops, I typically get responses such as the following:

- That is the rule, Samantha. You need to sit on your name label.
- Everyone sits on their name labels, Samantha, at circle time.
- It's not fair if you don't sit on your label, because the other children will be sitting on theirs.

Another approach to this situation could be for the teacher to think about what Samantha is really saying. What is behind Samantha's insistence? Understanding Samantha will help guide the teacher's response. Is Samantha simply being manipulative, controlling, and oppositional? Possibly. It is normal and developmentally appropriate for preschoolers to attempt to control as much as they can in their lives, in an effort to learn their boundaries and capabilities. At the same time, there could be a variety of other reasons. Perhaps Samantha wants to feel special, to be recognized. Perhaps she has very good control of her body and does not need the name label to help her function well at circle time.

If the teacher decides that, in fact, Samantha could probably behave appropriately at circle time without the name label, my suggestion would be to grant her wish. When I suggest this exception, teachers get very nervous! Usually, they worry that if they make an exception for Samantha, all the other children will want to throw away their name labels, the teacher will lose all authority in the classroom, and chaos will reign.

Consider this: If, at this time of the school year, all of the children no longer need the name labels at circle time, just get rid of them for everyone. If some of the children still really need the name labels, then allow the exception for Samantha and continue the name labels for the rest of the group. It is not the rule itself that is most important; the goal or purpose behind the rule is the most important aspect. If a child can meet the goal or purpose of the rule without abiding by the rule itself, then the rule is unnecessary for that child.

In many situations, a teacher can make an exception in a way that is not all that noticeable to the other children and does not have to be discussed in the group. In this case, the teacher could speak individually to Samantha, saying, "You know, Samantha, I think you're right that you could probably manage very well at circle time without the name label. Let's take it off and see how it goes. This can be your plan at circle time." The other children may not even notice the change. If other children notice and ask about the change, the teacher can say, "Samantha asked me to remove her name label because she doesn't need it to find and stay in her space on the rug at circle time anymore. I've noticed that for many of the children, the name label is still very helpful as they keep quiet bodies at circle time, so I am going to keep the labels for most of the group. Sometimes it's okay to have a special plan, and we can make different special plans for other children when they need them."

While it is reasonable to have certain behavioral guidelines and expectations for children in a preschool setting, it is not reasonable to have automatic consequences for breaches of these guidelines. At a workshop I gave on the importance of being a reflective teacher, one brave participant volunteered her rule on physical aggression: "If you hit, you sit!" meaning that if a child hits another child, the aggressor must leave the play area and sit down by herself for a period of time. The positive aspect of this idea is that it establishes a consistent message that physical aggression is never acceptable and will be addressed. However, that approach to hitting is not a productive one. Teachers may hope that when a child is forced to sit down for a while, she will reflect upon her behavior, but this is not usually the case. The child is more likely to feel angry and resentful and to bide her time until she can return to play, having learned no new skills to help her manage the next potentially frustrating or challenging situation.

Children hit their peers for a variety of reasons, and each situation is different. One child may be frustrated that he was not quick enough to line up first for outdoor time, so he pushes his peer. Another child hits a child who has insisted on using all of the large blocks when she wanted some for her own project. A third child hits a peer in the dramatic play area because the child had grabbed the broom out of his hand when he was playing with it. Each one of these situations could be ripe for problem solving and learning, based on the details of the situation. For children who repeatedly resort to using physical aggression as a response to their peers, a teacher will need to work with a team to develop an individualized intervention plan based on a comprehensive exploration of the particular child's personal situation and needs. Such plans are discussed in detail in the next chapter.

The teacher calls the children to the rug for story time, and one little boy, Nick, has a difficult time keeping his body quiet. At first, the teacher simply reminds Nick to keep his body to himself, a reasonable intervention on her part. Nick is quiet for a few moments and then begins to shift around on the rug again, bothering his neighbors. The teacher firmly tells him that he needs to stop bothering his neighbors because he is making it hard for the other children to listen to the story. Again, Nick is quiet for a few moments but cannot seem to maintain his focus and begins to bother the other children.

Frustrated by Nick's behavior, the teacher calls him up to the front of the rug area and directs him to sit by himself, in front of the whole group, facing the wall.

When I present this example in my workshops, teachers usually react pretty negatively to it. Hearing this story, it is easy to empathize with the young child who has been humiliated. At the same time, one can understand the teacher's frustration with this child, as his behavior was distracting and disruptive and did interfere with the activity the teacher was presenting to the group.

When I ask the participants at my workshops for suggestions of other interventions the teacher might have made with Nick, they frequently have some very good ideas:

- Have Nick sit on a chair rather than on the rug, to help contain his body better.
- Have him hold a fidget, such as a squishy ball, to give him something to do.
- Ask Nick to be the page turner for the story, thus taking him away from his peers and offering him the opportunity to be helpful and feel special.
- Delineate the space on the rug more clearly by creating a circle or square out of colored masking tape so that Nick has a clearly marked sitting spot.

Sometimes, teachers express concern in response to these options, asking, "Isn't that just rewarding bad behavior?" After all, Nick was bothering his neighbors, and next thing you know, the teacher offers him the special opportunity to be the page turner. The goal is not to make Nick pay for his mistaken behavior. The goal is to help him learn to behave appropriately.

Sometimes teachers also worry that the other children will behave poorly in the hopes of receiving a similar type of "reward." Avoiding this outcome is entirely dependent on how the teacher presents her intervention. The teacher can simply explain to Nick and his classmates, for example, "Nick, it's clear you're having a hard time keeping a quiet body today. I think it might help you to have something active to do. How about if you help us by being our page turner for the story today?" This explanation probably will suffice for most children in the class. If one or two feel like they also would like to be page turners, the teacher can respond, "That's a great idea! Today Nick really needs to use his body in a way that will help rather than hurt, so I think he needs to be our page turner. You are doing a great job of keeping a quiet body so that we can all listen to the story. I will let you be a page turner tomorrow." This response acknowledges the children's wishes to also have a special role. At the same time, she is supporting their good functioning by commenting on how they are keeping quiet bodies during circle time, and she is explaining why this job is especially important for Nick, thus encouraging empathy on the part of the other children.

The rule in a classroom is that all blocks must be put back in the bins at the end of free play time. A group of boys has been building some wonderful vehicles out of LEGOs. When clean-up time arrives, they hide their vehicles rather than put them back in their proper container.

One could certainly understand if the teacher was irritated by their behavior. After all, they have defied her request to clean up and are not following the class rule. The next children in the block area will not have as many blocks to play with. However, by reflecting on what may be behind the boys' behavior, the teacher may choose to respond in a different way.

They have spent a lot of time working on their creations. Perhaps they simply do not want to give up the constructions they are so proud of. I have presented this situation to many groups and have received some creative suggestions:

● Take a photograph of the vehicles the boys had constructed, and post the photographs in a place of honor in the classroom.

- Have the boys present their vehicles to their classmates at group time, explaining what they made and how they made them. Then, they can put the blocks away.
- Save the vehicles on a classroom shelf for a day, so that the boys can see them again before returning them to the bin.

All of these options would accomplish the goal of getting the LEGOs back into the container in time for others to have a chance to use them. They also focus on recognizing and appreciating the boys' creativity, rather than focusing on their refusal to put the blocks away in a timely fashion. Often, behavioral issues can be stopped before they start. Planning ahead will set the children up for success.

Maria and Rose love to play chasing games outside; they could do that all day. When the teacher rings the bell at the end of outdoor time, the children are supposed to line up at the door. Instead, Maria and Rose run to the back of the playground and hide. The first time this happens, the teacher has to ask the assistant director to gather the girls from the back of the yard so that she can stay with the rest of the class. The teacher tells the girls in no uncertain terms that they must come to the door when they hear the bell. The second time, the teacher tells the girls they must sit on the porch and miss part of play time because they have not cooperated with the rule.

After that, the teacher thinks of a better way to handle the situation. Just before she rings the bell, she puts an arm around Maria and Rose's shoulders and says, "Guess what, ladies! The bell is about to ring, and you two can be the first ones to get to the door today! We can go together!" There is no opportunity for them to run away because the teacher has an arm around each girl. She makes getting to the door first something fun, rather than a sad ending to outdoor play.

By going to the girls before the behavior has occurred, the teacher prevents the girls from running away and turns a negative behavior into a positive one. She encourages them to be the first ones in line, helping them feel special and important in a more productive way.

There are many opportunities for teachers to head off such difficult behaviors through reflecting on the motive behind the behavior and then planning ahead for success. To be successful in focusing on goals rather than on consequences, a teacher must understand that fairness means meeting the needs of each child and must recognize that not all children's needs are the same. When the goal is productive functioning in the classroom instead of suffering for wrongdoing, problem-solving approaches become the natural tendency and everyone in the classroom benefits.

Questions for Reflection

1. How do you define *fairness*?
2. What is your response to the notion that teachers must focus on the goals classroom rules are meant to achieve, rather than on the rules themselves?
3. Think of a child in your classroom who engages in a disruptive or otherwise challenging behavior. What do you think the child may be trying to achieve with this behavior? What kind of problem-solving approach might be useful with that child?
4. What do you think of the example of Nick, the child who bothered his peers on the rug? Do you think allowing him to be page turner was rewarding bad behavior, or do you see it in a different way? What would you have done in response to Nick in that situation?
5. If you feel it is appropriate, edit your list of goals and values that you created in Chapter One.

Individualizing Interventions

What is a teacher to do when a child frequently lashes out at peers, does not respond to the teacher's requests or limits, and is taking up an inordinate amount of the teacher's time and focus to keep him and the other children safe? This is the kind of challenge that most teachers dread. People who choose to work with young children find the energy and curiosity that children exhibit to be charming and invigorating. They enjoy connecting with the children and getting to know each one individually. Yet, when faced with a child whose behavior goes beyond run-of-the-mill disruptions and instead demands tremendous attention and time, the very underpinnings of the teacher's attachment to her work come into question. She may feel frustrated or angry with the child whose behaviors are so demanding, and she may feel unable to meet the child's needs. In these situations, creating individualized intervention strategies is critically important.

Developmentally appropriate practice tells us that it is essential for teachers and programs to accept each child at the level at which he is functioning. Schools must be ready for children as much as children need to be ready for school. This kind of flexibility and adaptability is one of the great advantages of high-quality early childhood programs: Teachers work hard to create a community that welcomes each child, despite possible behavioral challenges. However, in his research through the Yale Child Study Center, Walter Gilliam found that state-funded preschool programs expel more than three times as many children as do public schools serving kindergarten through twelfth grade. He also found that the expulsion rates vary across preschool settings: Faith-based, for-profit, and other community-based programs expel at rates significantly higher than those of Head Start or school-based programs. Gilliam found that, among preschools that received regular behavioral and mental health consultation, the expulsion rate was much lower. This indicates that when preschool teachers receive the training and support they need to help improve young children's behaviors, they do so in ways that enable children to succeed in their preschool settings.

The Individuals with Disabilities Education Act (IDEA) is a federal law put in place to ensure that children with diagnosed special needs have access to the services they need to be successful. Many children who have special needs are diagnosed at birth or shortly thereafter; however, some children's special needs are diagnosed later, often during the preschool years. When a child is diagnosed with a special need, a plan—an Individual Family Services Plan (IFSP) for babies and toddlers or an Individualized Education Program (IEP) for older children—must be created to address that child's needs.

The type of plan developed for that child is different from an individualized intervention strategy developed for a child who exhibits challenging behavior but does not have a diagnosed special need. In either case, however, a carefully thought-out plan will enable families, teachers, and staff to work together to provide the best possible support for the child's success. In this chapter, we explore strategies for working with young children who exhibit challenging behaviors but do not have a diagnosed special need that requires an IFSP or IEP.

Throughout this book, we have explored ideas for connecting with families and using reflective strategies to understand and help young children succeed. Families are an important resource for working with children who exhibit challenging behaviors. Through a trusting relationship, teachers can have honest conversations with family members regarding difficult behaviors. When parents trust and feel accepted by their child's teachers, they are more likely to engage positively with teachers to explore and address children's behaviors at school. Additionally, when families have a bond with their child's teachers and know their intentions are positive, they are more likely to follow up on suggestions for outside evaluations or interventions.

Building understanding of the underlying conflicts, needs, and possible family challenges that result in challenging behaviors helps build teachers' motivation and energy for working to help such children succeed. Teachers often worry that creating individualized strategies for some children is unfair to the other children in the classroom. Frequently, children who exhibit challenging behavior take up a lot of the teacher's time, and teachers may think that, with an individualized strategy, even more energy will be invested in a difficult child. Instead, with a well-thought-out intervention in place, the teacher will find that she has more time to interact with the other children in the classroom.

Some essential components and prerequisites must be in place for this kind of individualizing to be done successfully.

- Be flexible and assess the child's ability to function appropriately within the range of developmentally appropriate expectations.
- Recognize that challenging behaviors are not typically a child's attempts to manipulate and may not be within the child's control.
- Be patient and stay with an individual strategy for a period of time, without expecting the child's behavior to improve immediately. In most cases, individualized strategies should be implemented for a period of weeks rather than days.
- Establish a sense of community in the classroom, acknowledging that individuals differ in ability. Sometimes children need special plans, and that is okay.
- Understand that everyone has the right to have her needs met, and not all needs are the same.

Other elements necessary for making this practice successful are adequate, close supervision and support from supervisors and directors. The people who advise and guide teachers need to help them create appropriate individualized intervention strategies, support them in following through with the plans once developed, and help them review the effectiveness of the strategies and revise the plans as needed. Having supportive colleagues and mentors makes creating and implementing these strategies much easier.

Often, teachers worry that they must essentially study their classroom list each week and come up with special plans for each child in the classroom. Most children will not need a special plan at all; however, for those who struggle, special intervention strategies can support them as they learn to function sucessfully in the classroom.

There are lots of ways to individualize interventions. At the most intensive end of the continuum is asking family members, the teacher(s), an administrator, and, if necessary, a mental health professional to construct a formal intervention plan. In severe cases, that might include bringing in an additional adult to help supervise and monitor a child whose

Children who exhibit challenging behavior take up a lot of the teacher's time, and teachers may think that creating an individualized strategy will require that even more energy must be invested in a difficult child. Instead, a well-thought-out intervention will give the teacher more time to interact with the other children in the classroom.

behavior is so difficult that it is hard to keep the child and the rest of the children safely engaged in play. Some programs have funds that enable them to bring in additional help. Other programs will ask floater teachers or assistant directors to come into classrooms during times of day that may be especially difficult for certain children. At the other end of the continuum, a teacher can give a child a specific task, job, or opportunity that is not offered to the other children, a "special plan" that is devised just for her. The idea of individualizing interventions must be part of the classroom culture and seen as an option for any child, not just for the children who exhibit extremely challenging behaviors.

When a teacher takes the time to observe a child, reflect on his behavior, and understand the needs that the child is meeting through this behavior, she can better determine if simple methods of intervention are needed or if the behavior warrants the creation of a specific intervention strategy. Carefully thought-out and designed individual intervention strategies enable children to function more successfully; therefore, the teacher is less likely to need to intervene and handle challenging behaviors throughout the day.

Individualized intervention strategies serve several important functions. They can provide additional structure or extra support to help a child function more appropriately, teach a child to engage appropriately with his peers, allow a child additional space or time to conform to group norms, or provide an alternative to group expectations that may not work for every child. Proactive intervention can help teachers avoid power struggles and conflicts. Also, strategies can help anchor a child who has a hard time settling into activities. All forms of intervention have the goal of restoring the child to or helping him attain a higher, more appropriate level of functioning in the classroom. The hope is that, over time, a special strategy will no longer be necessary.

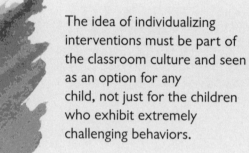

The idea of individualizing interventions must be part of the classroom culture and seen as an option for any child, not just for the children who exhibit extremely challenging behaviors.

Strategies for Structure and Support

Some children seem to fall apart during transitions or free-choice time. When productively engaged in play, they can manage pretty well because the structure of the play creates a sense of confidence and competence for them. When the play ends, however, some children just lose themselves during the time in between planned activities. For young children, that period in between can feel threatening. Sometimes children wander around the room aimlessly or behave aggressively toward others because of their anxiety. For such a child, having a teacher walk her through the transition can help her stay focused and feel secure. There are a number of ways to accomplish this:

- The teacher could invite the child to be the teacher's partner at clean-up time.
- The teacher could ask the child to assist him as the children gather their belongings to go outside.
- The teacher could give the child a special task, such as being the door holder, passing out napkins at snack time, being a page turner at circle time, and so on.

There are a myriad of ways that teachers can help children feel important and special. These mild interventions can also support social learning in children who struggle to engage appropriately with their peers.

Three-and-a-half-year-old Trey frequently hits and pushes his peers. If he is playing with the trains, for example, and another child walks by, Trey might push him away. If Trey wants to join children who are building with blocks, he might walk over and take a block out of a child's hands or hit the child. This behavior exasperates his teacher, who says that his behavior seems to come out of nowhere.

By systematically observing and reflecting on Trey's behavior, his teacher learned quite a lot. Trey does not know how to approach peers to join in play, and he may see peers as a threat to what he is doing by himself. To help Trey learn more appropriate ways of engaging with his peers, his teacher came up with some ideas. She noticed that Trey often engages in aggressive behavior during free-play time. She walked Trey over to the play area each day and talked with him about which area he wanted to explore. Then, she either helped him take out materials and find a protected space where he could play by himself or, if he seemed interested in group play, helped him approach other children. When she helped him approach other children, she gave him the words to use to ask if he could play. When he wanted to work on a project by himself, she gave him the words to inform other children that he was working by himself and did not want to play with anyone right now. While this individualized strategy initially did take up some of the teacher's time, it was much less disruptive to the flow of free play than when the teacher had to frequently respond to Trey's inappropriate behaviors.

Strategies for Alternatives to Group Expectations

Some children struggle to meet classroom expectations. While such behaviors may seem, on the surface, to be defiant, often an underlying need is driving the behavior.

Four-year-old Olivia frequently becomes deeply involved in her art explorations using all kinds of materials. When she hears the clean-up song, she simply loses her cool. Sometimes she cries; sometimes she yells, "No! I'm not done!"

Olivia is a child who becomes immersed in her explorations and who struggles with moving from one activity to another. For such a child, even the five-minute warning that teachers often give before a transition is not enough to help her let go. Olivia's teacher decided that it might help if he set up an egg timer for Olivia and gave her an additional two minutes after the other children had begun to clean up. This approach gave Olivia a chance to complete her work with a little more sense of control. She was much calmer and was able to move into the transition successfully.

Many preschool programs incorporate jobs charts to help children learn how to function within the classroom community. Generally, children enjoy doing different tasks, rotating among them each week. When one job ends, they are happy to move on to the next task. Occasionally, however, a child will struggle with giving up a job she enjoys. Often, young children do not know how to express the way they feel and may behave in disruptive ways.

Carrie is three years old and loves being the lunch helper. This job rotates weekly, so that each child can be a lunch helper for one week every couple of months or so. In between, the children have other classroom jobs to do. Carrie, however, loves being able to leave circle time a bit early to go and be lunch helper. When it is not her turn to help, she is miserable. She cries and has difficulty attending to the teacher and participating in activities with the other children.

Being lunch helper made Carrie feel special, and the other classroom jobs simply were less appealing to her. Her teacher tried hard to comfort her each week when it was not her turn to be lunch helper, but circle time was becoming quite challenging. She frequently found that she had to address Carrie's disappointment and frustration.

Thinking creatively, she decided to find a task that might capture Carrie's interest. She asked her to water the two classroom plants, each one on a different day of the week. She spoke with her co-teacher, who was in charge of setting up lunch, about supervising Carrie's watering of these plants, and he agreed. Then, she presented the plan to Carrie, saying, "Carrie, I've been thinking a lot about circle time. I know it's really hard for you to have a good time at circle time when it's not your turn to be lunch helper. I don't always remember to water our two classroom plants. It would be really helpful if you could water one of them on Tuesday and the other one on Thursday. What do you think? Would you be willing to have this special plan?"

Not surprisingly, Carrie loved the plan! Her teacher showed her how to put water in the watering can and how to use it. The teacher made a calendar with simple pictures for Carrie to look at so she would know when it was her day to water. She loved checking her own special weekly calendar each day, loved having an adult help her get the water into the watering can, loved leaving circle time early a couple of days a week, and especially loved the feeling of importance that this task gave her. Even though she did not do the job every day, it worked wonderfully to help Carrie feel valued in the classroom.

Strategies for Independent Choices

Because many preschoolers are able to make independent choices for play activities, teachers sometimes forget that this is a high expectation for this age group. Children are expected to look around the room, choose an activity area that seems appealing, take out the materials, play appropriately in the area, and interact appropriately with the other children in the area. When they are finished with the activity, they must look around the room again and find another area that looks appealing, use the play materials there appropriately, and interact with the children in that area. This is a lot for preschoolers to accomplish! Therefore, it should not be surprising that some children find these expectations too difficult and need additional help to navigate the classroom and engage in play.

Three-year-old Jovan has a hard time engaging in activities. He wanders rather aimlessly around the classroom, occasionally taking out a toy or puzzle and playing with it for a few minutes, then wandering around again. The teacher gets frustrated with Jovan at times because he does not really spend much quality time with any of his choices. Reminding Jovan to finish his puzzle does not get much of a response, and the teacher finds herself frequently asking Jovan to put away the games or toys he has left out around the classroom.

After discussing the problem with her supervisor, his teacher conducted some focused observations of Jovan. She noticed that he did not seem to know how to invest in the activities he took out. She made a plan to have a private dialogue with Jovan each day regarding what he might like to play with. She would make a couple of suggestions for him, based on her understanding of his apparent play preferences; for example, she would offer, "Jovan, there's a really fun new car puzzle in the rack today that you might like to try. Or, you might enjoy exploring painting with leaves. Which would you like to do first?" By asking Jovan which activity he would like to do first, she limited his choices and helped him focus.

When he chose, she walked over to that area with him and helped him get started. After a few minutes, she said, "Wow, Jovan! This puzzle is not an easy one, but you are really figuring it out! I need to check on what's happening in the dramatic play area right now, but I can watch you with my eyes. When you finish the puzzle, please bring it to show me!"

By taking a few moments to get a child started in an activity, the teacher acted as an anchor to help the child invest and engage. Once the child was engrossed in the exploration, the teacher kept the connection with the child alive by telling him she would watch him even when she is not sitting with him.

Most children in preschool classrooms function well without any sort of special plan. However, for the children who seem to struggle with engaging in activities, making transitions, or initiating and sustaining peer relationships, special intervention strategies can support those children as they learn to function successfully in the classroom.

Strategies for Challenging Behaviors

Most children function successfully within the preschool setting with occasional support, as necessary, from an individual intervention strategy. However, sometimes children exhibit behaviors that are physically or emotionally dangerous or destructive to others or that disrupt the classroom in such a way that other children are unable to learn. To figure out which kinds of behavior require more extensive individualized intervention plans, it is helpful to return to Dan Gartrell's description of young children's misbehavior as mistaken behavior. In his book *A Guidance Approach for the Encouraging Classroom*, Gartrell describes three levels of mistaken behavior:

- Level One: Experimentation
- Level Two: Socially Influenced
- Level Three: Strong Unmet Needs

The first level involves young children's experimentation with different kinds of behavior to see both how it feels and also what kinds of responses they receive from adults and peers. This would include behavior they may observe in others and try out for themselves. The second level includes the kinds of behaviors children see in their popular peers, the ones who seem to have some leadership or favored status in the classroom. They may, for example, join in teasing a child or rushing to the door to be first in line after seeing a peer do so. Socially influenced behavior can include positive behaviors as well, such as creative thinking regarding ideas for play, patience, kindness, or generosity. When socially influenced behavior is harmful, however, the teacher must address it to help children understand why such behavior is unacceptable. Once children learn why certain behaviors are not wise choices, they frequently will cease the behavior. These first two levels of mistaken behavior are generally easy to manage because they are not deeply ingrained in the child and are, therefore, more amenable to modifying based on the response they receive.

The third level of mistaken behavior arises out of strong unmet needs and comes from a psychological dynamic that is occurring inside the child's psychosocial self. It is not simply an experiment or a reflection of something the child has observed in a peer. And, it is not the kind of behavior that will change simply as a result of one or two explanations, diversions, or conversations with the teacher. Gartrell's description implies that the child is not simply attempting to cause trouble or be difficult in some way. This type of behavior requires an individualized intervention plan that is designed specifically to address the particular child's needs and vulnerabilities.

A carefully thought-out intervention plan is a useful tool to help a child learn more appropriate behaviors. Not using one actually enables more difficult behaviors as the child grows older.

I consulted at a program where I observed a two-and-a-half-year-old boy who was acting quite bossy. He was one of the oldest children in his class and was about to transfer into the preschool classroom. He had good verbal skills, but he used them in unkind ways at times. He grabbed things from the other children, told them their artwork was ugly, and once, when the teacher was not looking, actually painted on another child's back. The teacher was very attentive and talented, yet she felt extremely frustrated with this child. She tried intervening, redirecting, and teaching him kind words to use when he wanted something. Despite her best efforts, his mistaken behavior continued, and she was at her wit's end. This boy's mom was about to give birth to a sibling, which may have accounted for some of his difficult behavior. The parents also had a hard time setting limits with their son, and he often ruled the roost at home, according to the teacher.

The Insightful Teacher

We agreed that this little guy needed help to interrupt the pattern of aggressive behavior he had difficulty controlling. While some aggressive behavior is within the range of normal behavior in two-year-olds, the parents and teacher must show the child alternative ways of interacting and must reinforce that aggression cannot be allowed. We came up with a plan.

When he used mean words or ungentle hands with another child, the teacher first would intervene with suggestions for alternative words or actions he could choose that would be acceptable in the situation. If the boy was too excited or overstimulated to take in the teacher's input in the moment, she would direct him to an area where he could be by himself for a little while. He could continue to play at an activity that he enjoyed, but he could not play alongside other children until he was ready to use kind words and gentle hands. After a few minutes by himself, he would call out, "Teacher, I'm ready to use kind words and gentle hands now!" and the teacher would send him off to rejoin his friends. His behavior gradually improved.

Not long after this consultation and intervention, the staff met to discuss this child's transition to a preschool class. The lead teacher in the preschool classroom did not think that the intervention plan would be needed in his classroom. We all hoped that this child's behavior might improve now that he would be with bigger, older, and more sophisticated children who would model better social skills.

More than a year later, I observed the preschool class, and I saw that this now four-year-old boy had become quite the tyrant in the classroom. He teased and taunted other children, and the teacher patiently and endlessly reminded him not to do this. The teacher would redirect the boy to another area of the classroom, where he would usually simply start a problem with a new group of children. The teacher was enabling the boy's disruptive and aggressive behavior. It was sad to see how this boy's behavior had deteriorated, when he had responded well to the interventions we had devised. His behavior pattern was now consistent, so a carefully planned, comprehensive intervention strategy aimed at helping him learn how to change his bullying interactions and to connect more constructively with his peers was needed.

What was key in the original intervention plan was the manner in which it was implemented. Had his first teacher spoken to the child in a punitive way and sent him to play by himself because he was being naughty, the approach would have been less effective. She needed to intervene and check whether, with a little adult help, this little boy could improve his behavior and use more appropriate words and interactions. She suggested different words he could say or a different action he could choose to meet his needs. Sometimes, the teacher's suggestions were helpful and the child could use them in the moment, so that his play alongside others could continue. At other times, he was not amenable to such suggestions, and the teacher had to give him some time to play alone so that he could be ready to rejoin his friends in a calmer way.

This example demonstrates that there are times when a child does need to experience an individualized intervention strategy to learn how to change a misguided behavior. Even in such circumstances, the intervention strategies should be designed in a way to actually help the child learn rather than to make him suffer. Having a child play by himself at something he likes is a way of providing an outlet if a child is having difficulty cooperating with others. It also gives a clear message that being hurtful with others will not be tolerated.

Designing an Individualized Intervention Strategy

To understand what a child's needs and vulnerabilities are, the teacher must do some focused observations and often must consult with the family and colleagues. During this exploration period, the goal is to watch for patterns. Ask questions such as the following:

- Does the behavior occur more at certain times of day?
- Does it occur more often with certain children?
- Does it occur more often at transitions?
- Has an event occurred in the child's life that may be impacting her behavior?

Frequently, when teachers first notice these difficult behaviors, they may appear to "come out of the blue," with no rhyme or reason. However, what drives the behavior is usually a need that the child does not know how to meet in a productive way.

After doing some focused observations of the child and taking notes, a pattern typically does appear. Reflecting on the information gained through the exploration, observations, and discussions about the child, the teacher can shape an intervention strategy to help the child function more successfully. Even when she is not exactly sure what is driving a child's behavior, a teacher can develop a theory based on her knowledge of the child within the context of his development and family situation. Once the strategy is implemented, the teacher can adjust it as necessary to meet the child's needs. All of this requires commitment to helping the child function successfully. The teacher can empathize with the child and maintain the needed energy to carry out the intervention strategy when she views the child as simply trying to meet his needs.

Alex is physically intrusive with the children sitting near him at circle time. He interrupts the teacher as she attempts to lead a group activity, and he engages in silly, attention-seeking behaviors. His teacher has tried a number of interventions with him: keeping him near her, letting him be the page turner, and giving him a beanbag chair to sit in. None of these strategies has worked for long.

In an attempt to find an intervention for Alex, his teacher reflects on his behavior. She realizes that Alex engages in disruptive behaviors when he is required to sit in a group. She knows that he particularly enjoys puzzles, and this activity helps him stay focused and calm. She decides that having Alex sit at a table and work on puzzles near the circle time group will be a good plan for him.

While some preschoolers can sit and participate in large groups for twenty minutes or so, many cannot. Certainly children who have developmental lags will have more difficulties with this task, but even children who are developing typically may find large group times challenging. Teachers use a variety of strategies to support children's success at large group times. They may have the child sit next to an adult or even on an adult's lap, which may be helpful and reassuring for some children. For a child who may struggle with physical boundary issues, they may offer the child a chair to sit on rather than the rug. For children who have mild sensory integration challenges, a beanbag chair can be a good solution. For the child who seems to need to move rather than sit, being a page turner could be a helpful strategy. Others respond well to holding a Koosh ball or some other fidget. These are all appropriate and useful strategies for teachers to try in their attempts to support children.

However, occasionally none of these strategies quite does the trick for a particular child. In such a situation, the teacher must find an activity that the child can do well on his own, without direct adult supervision. Rather than rewarding "bad" behavior, offering an alternative activity helps a child meet a need and function more successfully in the classroom. The other children in the classroom are likely to accept the simple explanation that the child is "working on" a particular skill and has a special plan to help him.

In Alex's case, he struggles to focus within the large group. By having him work on a puzzle by himself but still close by the group, the teacher is setting Alex up for success. He can hear what is going on at circle time and can learn the songs and the new material that is presented there, while keeping himself occupied and quiet.

Children learn to be independent through having their dependency needs met. Alex can learn to increase his ability to sit quietly by meeting his need to have something to do on his own. After some time with this strategy, the teacher can have Alex gradually return to circle time with the group, first sitting next to an adult and staying for the first five minutes and then leaving to do puzzles, and gradually staying longer. By providing him with this outlet, the teacher allows time for him to internalize this necessary skill.

He may need this special plan for a month, or he may need it for many months. The teacher can assess how he is doing over time and can determine when and how to adjust or end the strategy.

By recognizing and planning for children's different skill and ability levels, teachers support their growth. They also build real community in the classroom when they help all children recognize that each child's needs differ at times and that accepting one another despite our varying strengths and vulnerabilities is a value.

Presenting the Strategy

Sometimes teachers can have the best of intentions in adopting a new approach to their work with children, but implementation can be a challenge. When presenting an individualized intervention strategy to a child, I prefer to call it a "special plan." Children can easily understand that, and all children like to feel special. A special plan, when labeled in this way, is less likely to be seen or experienced as some kind of consequence or punishment.

When presenting a special plan to a child, it is best to discuss it with the child when the child is calm and functioning well. A good way to begin the dialogue is to say, "You know, I've been thinking a lot about…." When you tell a child you have been thinking about him, he will receive a validating and supportive message and will know that he is important to you.

Focus on the positive behavior that you are looking for, rather than the difficult behavior the child has been exhibiting; for example,

> Alex, I've been thinking a lot about circle time. I know that sitting quietly at circle time is very hard for you. That is something that you are still working on. I also know that you do puzzles very well and that activity helps you be settled. I've decided that your special plan for circle time will be to sit at a table near the group and work on puzzles. That way, you can stay settled and still hear what is happening there. Over time, it will get easier for you to stay settled at circle time, too, and I know you will come back to the group and join us again.

In this way, the teacher holds out the expectation that the child will gain the ability to function more appropriately in the future, and she conveys this in a positive way.

How the special plan is presented is critically important to its success! If a teacher feels frustrated or irritated by a child's challenging behavior and presents the strategy in negative way, the child certainly will experience it as a sign of his failure and will feel humiliated and punished. Present the plan positively, with the expectation that it will benefit the child.

After presenting the strategy privately to Alex, the teacher can simply say to the other children,

> I've been thinking a lot about circle time and about how Alex has a hard time keeping his body quiet. This is something that he is working on. Doing puzzles is something that helps Alex stay settled, so I have decided that his special plan will be to do puzzles at the puzzle table while we have circle time. You guys do a great job of sitting and listening during circle time! After a while, when Alex doesn't need this plan anymore, he will come back and join us.

Sometimes teachers worry that somehow they may be violating a child's confidentiality if they speak about a child's behavior in front of others. While it is certainly important to respect confidentiality issues with families, talking about the strategy in this way does not tell the children anything they did not already know. The teacher has already spent time and energy working with Alex to help him settle down at circle time, so the children are already well aware of this issue. By explaining Alex's need for this special plan, the teacher is demonstrating her concern for helping him. The teacher is conveying the message that this plan is not a result of Alex being a "bad boy."

Occasionally, despite a teacher's best efforts at presenting the special plan in this way, other children may imitate the behavior that caused the need for the special plan, to see whether they can receive an exception as well. When this happens, the teacher simply can say, "You are doing what Alex did at circle time. That is not something you are working on. You know perfectly well how to sit and listen to stories, and I expect you to do it right now. If you do need a special plan sometime, I will make one for you. But, it will not be the same one that Alex needs." The teacher's confidence and firmness will go a long way toward quelling these attempts.

The Insightful Teacher

A teacher may encounter a child whose default response to an intervention is negative. Most children are interested and intrigued when the teacher brings in a new book to share or introduces a new material to the class. When a child consistently reacts in a negative way, figuring out how to handle such opposition can be quite challenging.

Marilyn is a four-year-old girl who has been in her preschool program for more than a year. She is quite bright and has a family who is committed to exposing their children to lots of enrichment experiences. They visit museums regularly and take interesting vacations filled with learning opportunities. Marilyn frequently makes disparaging comments about the classroom activities and materials.

Waking up from nap time is an especially difficult time of day for Marilyn. She usually wakes up cranky and often provokes peers with unkind comments such as, "You're in my way!" or "I don't want to play with you!" or "There's nothing fun to do here!" Her teacher realizes that Marilyn needs some time to get herself together after nap, but so far Marilyn has not cooperated with his efforts to help her.

He puts together a plastic shoebox with materials for Marilyn to use after her nap. He includes stickers and colored paper, some glitter pens, playdough, and a few miniature books made from construction paper stapled together, so Marilyn can make "stories" if she wants to.

He presents her special plan this way: "I've been thinking about nap time and how hard it is for you to wake up and settle into the afternoon. I know that a lot of the classroom materials aren't very interesting to you, so I put together a special box just for you to use. I will keep it in a special place for you. You probably won't like what I put together; it will probably be boring. If you want to use the materials, that's fine. If you decide you don't like them, I can just put them out for the other children to use. It's totally up to you. The box has your name on it, and it's on the table by the window if you want to look at it."

With most children, the teacher would present such a special plan with great enthusiasm, and the children would be quite pleased. However, Marilyn is usually resistant to the teacher's efforts, so he took a more laid-back approach. He stated his assumption that she probably would not be interested in what he had provided for her. He gave her the choice of whether to use the box of materials and told her that if she did not want them, that would be fine and he would simply offer them to the other children. This way, he let her know that if she wants to feel special by having these materials just for her, she can choose to accept them.

In this case, Marilyn did end up using the box. Perhaps it was the notion of being set apart from the other children, or perhaps it was her teacher's ingenuity in how he presented the special plan to her, but the intervention did help her have a better transition out of nap time.

Assessing the Strategy's Effectiveness

Sometimes, teachers make the mistake of believing that as soon as the child's behavior improves, the special plan can end because it is no longer needed. Frequently, however, the reason the child's behavior has improved is because he has had the support provided by the intervention strategy. If the plan is withdrawn too soon, the child's behavior is likely to deteriorate. It is always better to err on the side of continuing a special plan longer than a child really needs it than it is to end a strategy before a child is ready.

It can be difficult to determine when to end a specialized intervention strategy. How can a teacher know when the child no longer needs it? There is no easy answer. Making focused observations and reflecting on the circumstances of the child's behavior will help in determining any necessary adjustments to the plan.

I worked as an educational therapist in a school for children who have psychological challenges. The children were accustomed to some degree of individualized planning; however, because they did have emotional difficulties, they were more likely than typically developing children to be sensitive to issues of fairness.

David, a three-and-a-half-year-old, had significant problems with impulse control, often grabbing materials that he wanted from others. At snack time, David would shove his hand into the serving bowl full of pretzels and grab a handful, necessitating a new bowlful of snacks to avoid the spread of germs. The other children were frustrated by David's behavior and by having to wait for a new bowl of pretzels each day.

The underlying issue in his apparent greediness with toys, materials, and snacks was that David was worried about getting enough, about getting what he needed. I consulted with my supervisor and devised a strategy to reassure David that there would be enough for him at school, that he would be taken care of, and that his needs would be met.

Each morning, the snack tray included not only a large serving bowl of pretzels but also a separate small bowlful just for David. Not only would David have his own bowl during snack time, but he also would be able to keep his bowl in his locker all morning in case he felt he needed more to eat later on.

I presented the plan to the group, saying,

> I've been thinking a lot about snack time and about how hard it is for David to wait to be served. This is something he is working on, and he worries that there might not be enough for him. You guys don't worry about that, and you do a good job of waiting to be served at snack time. You eat what you want and then you're done, and that's a good thing. But this is harder for David, so I've decided that it would help him to keep his bowl in his locker in case he feels like he needs more snack later. This will help him learn that he will get enough at school. You know that when you need special plans, I make them for you, too. But you don't need this plan; this is what David needs.

There was very little arguing in response to the plan for David, and the children were pleased and relieved to learn that they would not have to wait for the snack tray to be returned to the kitchen for a new bowl each day. Because the other children did not worry that they might not get enough food, they did not really notice David's snack bowl in his locker all that often.

After about three weeks, I noticed that David's snack bowl was getting sent back to the kitchen at the end of the morning still full. He had not needed or wanted to eat more snacks; he had just needed to know that there would be enough for him. After a few more weeks of the snack bowl returning to the kitchen still full, I no longer kept a bowl in David's locker all morning. I did continue giving him his own bowl at snack time for quite a while, however.

Four-year-old Troy had a rather dangerous habit of putting inedible items into his mouth. He mouthed puzzle pieces, leftover cotton balls, and even small LEGOs. His teacher worked with him to use play materials appropriately, but the behavior seemed to be compulsive. The teacher wondered if Troy had a sensory oral issue that caused him to need to mouth objects.

An occupational therapist came to the school to observe Troy, and she agreed that he did have some mild sensory issues that caused him to crave oral stimulation. She suggested giving Troy a chew stick, a nondeteriorating rubber stick that a child can chew on safely. However, the chew stick had a bitter taste that Troy found very unappealing.

Troy's teacher talked with his supervisor, colleagues, and the director of the program to seek their approval for another idea that was a little controversial. When they agreed, he spoke with Troy's parents and sought their permission. Then he presented the new strategy to Troy.

He said, "You know, Troy, I've been thinking a lot about how much you like to have things in your mouth. I know you try hard not to put stuff in your mouth that isn't safe and isn't for eating, but sometimes it seems like you just can't help yourself. I've talked with your mom and dad and with Ms. Dayton, and I've decided that you need a new special plan to help you be safe about what you put into your mouth. Your plan will be to chew on a piece of sugar-free gum while you are playing at school, so that you can chew and still be safe by not putting toys and other things that aren't food in your mouth."

Troy loved the new plan. His parents brought in packs of sugar-free gum, which the teacher gave to Troy, half a piece at a time, during the periods when Troy was most likely to put things in his mouth.

Obviously, this was a highly controversial strategy. The staff had to discuss beforehand how they would handle possible reactions from the other children, and how they would be sure that Troy disposed of his gum properly. Many children like to chew gum but know that it is not allowed at school. How could it be fair or acceptable to allow one child to chew gum at school?

This is how the teacher explained Troy's plan to the other children:

I've been thinking a lot about making sure that children are safe at school. One thing that isn't safe is putting things in our mouths that aren't really food. This is something that Troy has a hard time with. Troy has the need to chew on things. You guys do a very good job of only putting food into your mouths and not chewing on other things that aren't safe, but Troy needs a special plan to help him be safe about what goes into his mouth. His special plan is to chew on a small piece of gum sometimes. We don't usually allow gum at school, but because it is helpful for Troy to be able to chew a lot, gum will help him be safe. His parents will bring the gum in for him, and it will be only for Troy. If you guys want to chew gum, too, you can ask your parents if they will let you chew gum after school.

In this program, the children were divided into small groups and assigned for much of the day to a special attachment teacher. Troy's attachment teacher decided that once in a while on a Friday afternoon he would allow the other children in his attachment group to chew gum with Troy. First, he got permission from the parents of the children in his subgroup, and he made this a rare and special occasion. In this way, he acknowledged that it is hard for children to see a friend have such a special privilege at school, especially when it involved a treat such as chewing gum. On a day-to-day basis, the other children did fine with understanding that Troy was the only child who could chew gum at school.

When noticeable exceptions are clearly explained to the children in a way that they can understand, they feel respected and understood. I believe that this way of treating children actually engenders their interpersonal generosity and acceptance.

Careful and thoughtful exploration of the child's situation and needs usually leads to helpful interventions. In the rare event that an individualized strategy leads to worsening behavior, which could happen if the planning somehow missed what the child actually needed, then the strategy should be reassessed quickly. Reflecting on the new information gathered by the child's negative behavioral response, the teacher can determine a new strategy. Teachers are not perfect, and mistakes in planning do occur. When this happens, revising the plan is the best practice and should happen right away.

If a child is not able to succeed even with careful and well-thought-out individual planning, then the staff will know that they have provided every possible support to encourage such success and that the child may need a different kind of setting.

Brittany, not quite three years old, entered a preschool program in April. She came to the program from a day-care home and joined a class ranging in age from three through five years. When the space had opened up, her mom had moved her to a preschool setting because she felt Brittany needed to be a "big girl."

Brittany exhibited a variety of challenging behaviors as soon as she arrived, which made the task of helping her adapt to her new setting especially difficult. The teachers observed that Brittany behaved more like a toddler than a preschooler. She was unfocused, flitted from one area of the room to another, and was easily overstimulated. When this happened, she would sometimes bite another child. The biting did not appear to be related to frustration or anger; it seemed to be a reflection of her lack of internal calm.

Brittany's teachers wondered whether allowing her to use a teething toy as a tension release might help her. Presenting this idea to her mother was not easy, however, as she wanted Brittany to be a "big girl" and not a baby anymore. Additionally, Brittany had entered the program so recently that there had not been much time to establish a trusting relationship between the staff and the mom. Brittany's teachers met with her mother, however, and she reluctantly agreed to the plan, as she was highly motivated to keep Brittany in preschool.

Brittany liked the teething toy, but it did not eliminate the biting. Sometimes she used her teething toy, but sometimes she still bit other children. Additionally, Brittany often used swear words in the classroom. The children found this quite fascinating and would laugh at what they knew was unacceptable behavior. Brittany also had a tendency to enter the bathroom when other children were there and to pull down the children's pants and giggle.

It is always somewhat demanding to bring a very young child into a preschool program late in the year, because the other children have been there for several months. In the fall, when there are many new children entering, the teachers tend to organize the classroom in a particular way. They set out fewer materials to avoid overwhelming the children with choices. They make a special effort to be particularly clear in explaining and supporting the children as they learn routines and norms, and they are generally tuned in to helping the children adapt to the new setting.

By April, the children are used to how the classroom operates. Many more materials are out and available for the children to access independently, and the teachers do not need to spend much time explaining or reminding children of basic classroom norms and expectations. Incorporating a particularly young child into the classroom at this time of year is challenging, even if the child is developing perfectly well in all areas.

In this case, the teachers explained to the other children that Brittany was younger than they were and that she had not yet learned about what words were okay to use at school and what words were not. They instructed the children to ignore Brittany when she used inappropriate language so that their responses to her would not be encouraging. This was a tough direction, but the other children did increase their skills in this area. To deal with Brittany's bathroom behavior, an adult closely supervised her at all times and did not allow her to be near the bathroom when another child was in it.

Although the other children rose to the occasion in a number of areas in relation to Brittany's difficult behaviors, Brittany was not able to make significant progress. Because biting is physically unsafe for others, the teachers could set only a limited timeframe for improvement. It was not possible to try different individualized interventions over a period of months to help Brittany stop biting others. The teachers were concerned about possible problems at home that might be leading to some of her excitable, overstimulated behavior, but the lack of an established relationship with the mother made it difficult to explore these concerns fully and work with the mother and child to make improvements.

After a few weeks of trying interventions to help Brittany settle down in the classroom, the teachers and director realized that the preschool setting was just too much for her to handle. Brittany seemed to need a smaller, more intimate setting where there was less stimulation and the opportunity for more one-on-one attention. Her mother was rather angry at the staff and disappointed that Brittany could not succeed in preschool at that time. Despite her dissatisfaction, the director was able to find a place for Brittany in a home day-care program with only a few children and led by an experienced and sensitive caregiver.

Sometimes, even with the best efforts, some children will not respond to individualized interventions in a way that allows them to succeed in a preschool setting. There were many factors that affected this less-than-satisfying outcome for Brittany, but the teachers and director knew that they had tried hard in a variety of ways to provide the additional supports that Brittany needed. It was just not enough for her at that time.

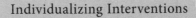

In the overwhelming majority of situations, preschoolers respond very well to individualized strategies that address their needs. Teachers need adequate support and supervision to carefully observe children and identify what is happening within the child or her environment that underlies challenging behaviors. When the school climate encourages such explorations and accepts that children come to school at various levels of functioning, individualized interventions go a long way toward enabling children to succeed.

Beyond simply helping a child succeed in a preschool setting, such planning also sends important messages to the other children in the classroom. Not only are they reassured that their own needs also will be met, but they learn to accept that we are all "working on" various skills and abilities. The message that every child has a place here creates a strong sense of community that stimulates children's kindness, generosity, and acceptance. These qualities can build their self-esteem as well as guide them to be more inclusive as they move on in their formal school experiences.

Questions for Reflection

1. Think of a few situations in which you used a "special plan" with a child in your classroom. Teachers often make minor exceptions for a child who needs extra help. In the situations you can think of, why did you make the plan, and how did it work?
2. After reading this chapter, can you think of any children in your classroom for whom a "special plan" might be useful in response to a recurrent difficult behavior? How would you arrive at such a plan, and what steps would you need to take to implement it?
3. What is your response to the idea of incorporating this approach into your repertoire of interventions with children and of making special plans for more than just the one or two children whose behaviors are especially challenging?
4. How might you help the children in your classroom with the concept that we are all "working on" something? Do you think this idea might be helpful to the children with whom you work? What other ways do you teach acceptance in your classroom?
5. If you feel it is appropriate, edit your list of goals and values that you created in Chapter One.

Putting It All Together

We want children to be curious and to love learning, to be self-confident, have strong social skills, make and keep friends, and to get along with everyone in the classroom, even with the children who might not be their favorites. We want to create classroom communities in which each child feels that he belongs, is valued, and has something to contribute. These skills build resilience in children—the confidence to master challenges and the tenacity to keep moving forward despite adversity. Teachers can have a profound influence on the lives of children. Recognizing the potential impact of their work on the children they serve can inspire teachers to reflect and find creative solutions to challenges in the classroom.

> Adults who have developed the resilience required to overcome extremely challenging personal histories tend to report that someone in their lives provided support and a model for interpersonal connection. Often, this person was a teacher—someone who made herself emotionally available to the child and modeled positive interpersonal connections.

As we have moved through this book, we have explored ways to develop insight through reflection. Think about your goals for your classroom. Consider how you will use the information you have learned to create a classroom environment that teaches and supports developmentally appropriate expectations. Think about how you will connect with the families who entrust their children to your care. And, reflect on how you will use your new repertoire of strategies and approaches to work with children in overcoming challenges and creating a healthy classroom community.

Scenarios for Practice

Following are a number of sample scenarios, each one representing a common classroom situation, dilemma, or challenge. Using the reflection process we have explored, consider how you would handle these situations by incorporating the strategies, techniques, and approaches we have discussed.

- Four-year-old Deanna has a disagreement with another child in the dramatic play area. Scott wants to pretend to be the pet dog, but Deanna wants him to be the baby instead. When Scott refuses, Deanna announces, "Then you can't come to my birthday party!" What do you think is happening here? What need is Deanna satisfying with her behavior? How can you address this situation?

- Three-year-olds Emma and Sylvia are painting in the art center. Emma accidentally bumps Sylvia's arm when she reaches for some paint. Sylvia yells, "You're stupid!" Emma starts to cry. Do you need to intervene? If so, what are your goals and what is your approach?

- Sammy wants to play with the big blocks. He runs to the block area, pushing Ramon down in the process. It is unclear whether Sammy intentionally pushed Ramon or perhaps ran into him. Should you intervene immediately or wait to see what happens next? If you do need to intervene, what are your goals and what is your approach?

- Three-year-old Maria walks into the dramatic play area and grabs a broom from Sara. She refuses to give it back when Sara objects. Sara, also three, attempts to grab it back, and the two girls begin struggling for control of the broom. How can you help them resolve this conflict?

- During circle time, four-year-old Maisey repeatedly interrupts the story with personal comments or questions while the teacher is reading to the group. The teacher reminds her that interrupting is not acceptable and that she needs to listen quietly or raise her hand if she wants to make a comment. Maisey continues to interrupt. What need do you think Maisey is meeting through this behavior? How could you help her participate in a less disruptive way?

- Samantha is an outspoken four-year-old who likes to be in charge of herself and others. She frequently ignores the teacher's announcement of clean-up time, continuing to play or simply wandering around the classroom rather than participating. When Samantha's teacher attempts to redirect her, she responds with "I don't want to!" or "I hate cleanup! No way!" How can you respond in a way to encourage Samantha's compliance?

- Michael is a young three-year-old who has recently entered a preschool program for the first time. He is having a hard time accepting other children coming into his space or touching toys that he is using. He either pushes or hits children when he feels they are getting in his way. Michael does not have any siblings and seems uncomfortable around groups of children. What can be done to help him function more successfully in the classroom?

- Reggie just turned three and entered a full-day preschool after having been cared for at home by a beloved babysitter for the past two years. He is struggling with intense separation feelings and sometimes cries loudly for long periods. In the afternoons, he frequently chooses to sit in a chair and look out the window, waiting for his mother to come and pick him up. What interventions might help Reggie master his feelings about separation? Create an intervention strategy to help him adapt to being in the preschool setting.

- Juan is a four-year-old boy who has been in the same preschool program for more than a year. He loves to play in a boisterous, physically adventurous way in the classroom and sometimes gets himself into dangerous situations, such as climbing on the block cabinet and jumping off. He knows the rules, but he seems unable to contain his need for physical movement and gross motor play. Develop a strategy to help Juan behave more safely and to channel his need for gross motor activity.

- Four-year-old Naomi and her friend Tonya are building a tall structure with large wooden blocks. It falls down, and Tonya is crying. You did not see what happened, but both girls are upset. How can you address this situation? Figure out a strategy that will focus on helping both girls feel better.

- Aaron and Sam, both three, are fighting over a fire truck in the classroom. Aaron says, "I had it, Sam! Let go!" Sam says, "It's my turn now! I need it!" What is your goal in addressing this situation? How will you intervene?

- Three-year-old Candy whines when she wants something from her teacher. Her teacher has talked with Candy about using a normal tone of voice, but she continues to whine. Frustrated, her teacher snaps, "Candy, that's enough of your baby talk! You need to act like a three-year-old or I'm not going to listen to you!" Candy immediately begins to cry. The teacher says, "When you settle down, we can talk," and moves to another part of the classroom. Candy eventually stops crying, but the teacher does not have a chance to resume a dialogue with her. What might the teacher do, if anything, the next day that might help her reconnect with Candy in a more positive way? What need might Candy be meeting through her behavior? Is there another way to respond to Candy's whining?

Questions for Reflection

1. What specific strategies in this book seem the most useful to you?
2. Choose a strategy that you plan to implement in your classroom. Name three steps you will need to take to make this happen.
3. Create a timeframe for implementation, and jot down your attempts to incorporate the strategies you have chosen. Remember, these new skills may take some time to develop. If at first you do not succeed, try again!
4. If you have found some of the information in this book especially useful, how might you communicate this to your colleagues or supervisors?

Questions to Add to Your Center's Intake Form

Your Child

Describe your child's personality (temperament, strengths, vulnerabilities, needs):

_____

_____

_____

_____

Does your child have any specific fears?

_____

_____

_____

Does your child have any nervous habits?

_____

_____

_____

Does your child have a transitional object, such as a special pillow, blanket, or stuffed animal? If so, is the child allowed to bring it to school?

_____

_____

_____

Check any of the following traits that apply to your child. If some only occur in certain situations, please describe those situations.

- [ ] active player
- [ ] quiet player
- [ ] affectionate
- [ ] stubborn
- [ ] difficult
- [ ] easygoing
- [ ] sensitive (to others' feelings)

- [ ] sensitive (has easily hurt feelings)
- [ ] leader
- [ ] follower
- [ ] friendly
- [ ] shy
- [ ] physically daring
- [ ] physically cautious

Any special circumstances for these behaviors:

_____

_____

_____

Child's best qualities:

_____

_____

_____

Child's most challenging qualities:

_____

_____

_____

Child's special interests or skills:

_____

_____

_____

Does your child enjoy listening to stories?

_____

_____

_____

How frequently do you read together?

_____

_____

_____

How much TV does your child watch?

_____

Does your child have a pet?

_____

If so, what is its name?

_____

What kinds of toys/play materials does your child enjoy?

_____

_____

_____

How does your child prefer to play (check all that apply)?

☐ by himself/herself?   ☐ with one other child

☐ with an adult?   ☐ in groups

Describe your child's attention span:

_____

_____

_____

Describe your child's energy level:

_____

_____

_____

What have you found works best in engaging your child's cooperation and positive behavior?

_____

_____

_____

How do you usually limit or discipline your child?

_____

_____

_____

How effective do your interventions feel to you?

_____

_____

_____

How do you respond when your child:
has a toilet accident:

_____

throws a temper tantrum:

_____

runs across the street:

_____

hits or lashes out at a parent:

_____

hits a playmate:

_____

Family Life

What holidays or special events or family traditions are celebrated in your family?

_____

_____

_____

What are some of your family's favorite foods?

_____

_____

_____

What do you hope school will do for your child?

_____

_____

_____

What do you want your child to get from his/her preschool experience?

_____

_____

_____

Additional comments:

_____

_____

_____

_____

_____

_____

_____

_____

_____

_____

_____

_____

_____

Resources

Boyd, Lizi. 1989. *Bailey the Big Bully*. New York: Viking Kestrel.

Brazelton, T. Berry, and Joshua Sparrow. 2002. *Touchpoints: Three to Six*. Boston: DaCapo Press.

Brazelton, T. Berry, and Joshua Sparrow. 2006. *Touchpoints: Birth to Three*, 2nd ed. Boston: DaCapo Press.

Deviney, Jessica, Sandra Duncan, Sara Harris, Mary Ann Rody, and Lois Rosenberry. 2010. *Inspiring Spaces for Young Children*. Silver Spring, MD: Gryphon House.

Edwards, Carolyn, Lella Gandini, and George Forman, eds. 2011. *The Hundred Languages of Children: The Reggio Emilia Experience in Transformation*, 3rd ed. Santa Barbara, CA: Praeger.

Erikson, Erik. 1959. *Identity and the Life Cycle: Selected Papers*. Madison, CT: International Universities.

Erikson, Erik. 1993. *Childhood and Society*, reissued ed. New York: Norton.

Faber, Adele, and Elaine Mazlish. 1987. *Siblings without Rivalry: How to Help Your Children Live Together So You Can Live Too*. New York: Norton.

Gardner, Howard. 1983. *Frames of Mind: The Theory of Multiple Intelligences*. New York: Basic Books.

Gartrell, Dan. 2013. *A Guidance Approach for the Encouraging Classroom*, 6th ed. Belmont, CA: Wadsworth-Cengage Learning.

Gilliam, Walter. 2005. *Prekindergarteners Left Behind: Expulsion Rates in State Prekindergarten Systems*. New Haven, CT: Yale University Child Study Center.

Gilliam, Walter. 2007. *Early Childhood Consultation Partnership: Results of a Random-Controlled Evaluation*. New Haven, CT: Yale University Child Study Center. Available online at www.chdi.org/admin/uploads/5468903394946c41768730.pdf.

Herner, John. 1998. "Teach." *Counterpoint*. Alexandria, VA: National Association of State Directors of Special Education.

Hunter, Tom. 2000. "Some Thoughts about Sitting Still." *Young Children*, 55(3): 50.

Isbell, Rebecca, and Pamela Evanshen. 2012. *Real Classroom Makeovers: Practical Ideas for Early Childhood Classrooms*. Lewisville, NC: Gryphon House.

Karst, Patrice. 2000. *The Invisible String*. Camarillo, CA: DeVorss & Co.

Kraus, Robert. 1971. *Leo the Late Bloomer*. New York: HarperCollins.

Lillard, Paula Polk. 1988. *Montessori: A Modern Approach*. New York: Schocken.

Minuchin, Salvador, and H. Charles Fishman. 1981. *Family Therapy Techniques*. Cambridge, MA: Harvard University Press.

Paley, Vivian. 1979. *White Teacher*. Cambridge, MA: Harvard University Press.

Penn, Audrey. 1993. *The Kissing Hand*. Washington, DC: Child Welfare League of America.

Vanderbilt University Center on the Social Emotional Foundations of Early Learning. 2013. "Resources: Practical Strategies for Teachers/Caregivers." Nashville, TN: Vanderbilt. Available online at http://csefel.vanderbilt.edu/resources/strategies.html.

Viorst, Judith. 1972. *Alexander and the Terrible, Horrible, No Good, Very Bad Day*. New York: Antheneum Books for Young Readers.

Winnicott, Donald. 1990. *Home Is Where We Start From: Essays by a Psychoanalyst*. New York: Norton.

Index

Mindset, 20

Mistaken behavior, 100

Mistrust, trust versus, 23–24

Music area, 47

N

Nap time, 68–69

P

Peace table, 92

Peer modeling, 55

Peers

cooperating with, 84–86

negotiating play and navigating conflicts, 86–91

Play

conflicts and negotiating, 86–91

cooperative, 38–41

Problem-solving skills, 91–98

Q

Quiet area, 47

R

Reflection

See also Insight

role of, 10–11

Reggio Emilia movement, 49

Respect, 59

S

Scheduling and transitions, 54–56

Science area, 46

Self-assessment and planning, 11–13

Self-regulation, 34–35, 79

Sensory area, 46

Separation, 29–31, 64–68

Shame and doubt, autonomy versus, 25–32

Sharing, 31–32, 41–43

Sick children, 69–70

Squirming children, 103–104

Social-emotional skills

cooperating with peers, 84–86

goals, 79

impulse control and developing vocabulary, 80–84

negotiating play and navigating conflicts, 86–91

problem-solving skills, 91–98

Story dictation and dramatization, 97

Storytelling, 97–98

Strengths, 14–17

T

Terrible twos, 26–27

Toys, selecting and organizing, 49–51

Transitions, 54–56

intervention strategies, 111–112

Trust

building, 64–68

versus mistrust, 23–24

V

Validate, Suggest, Depart, Acknowledge approach, 87–88

Values

communicating, 13–14

identifying, 10

Vanderbilt University Center on the Social and Emotional Foundations for Early Learning, 82

Vocabulary development, 80–84

The Insightful Teacher